T0265635

Advance Praise for *Call Me an American*

"The impassioned words in *Call me An American* are reflective of a great patriot whose life journey is a triumph of the human spirit in the face of tremendous adversity. Hung Cao's journey—as a refugee, a United States Naval Officer on the battlefield, and now—should inspire every American to stand courageously for our great nation and her founding ideals in the face of an insidious, ideological agenda that seeks to destroy the American dream. Hung Cao reminds the reader of what is the exceptionalism that makes our country unique, that beacon of light to the world, which we all must fight for and defend. *Call Me an American* should be required reading for all, young and old alike.

—Mark R. Levin

"Hung Cao's remarkable and inspiring story of how his family survived the defeat in Vietnam, overcame the adversity of having to flee communism, and established themselves in a new land of opportunity and freedom is a stunning tribute both to his family and to the America he served in the military. Hung Cao is the kind of energetic, intelligent, and courageous leader who will make America a better country. His book is a testimonial to those qualities."

—Speaker Newt Gingrich

"*Call Me an American* is a brilliant clarion call for our nation's future! Hung Cao—a shining example of a new 'Greatest Generation' rising up from decades of war—has given us a vision for American greatness. This book is essential reading for all those who truly care about the future of the USA. This is a road map for us, not just to survive, but to thrive. As we love our nation, as we love our children, as we love our way of life: read and heed!"

—Lt. Col. Dave Grossman USA (Ret.),
Author of *On Killing, On Combat,*
and *On Spiritual Combat*

"Hung Cao's life is an example of the true American dream. From immigrant to decorated naval officer, Cao's story, along with his love of God and country, will inspire every reader! His life experience brings a fresh perspective on what it truly means to be a 'proud American.'"

—Pastor Gary Hamrick,
Sr. Pastor, Cornerstone Chapel

CALL

ME

AN

AMERICAN

CALL ME AN AMERICAN

REFUGEE TO PATRIOT:
LESSONS LEARNED FOR
A STRONG AMERICA

HUNG CAO

WITH APRIL LAKATA CAO

A REPUBLIC BOOK
ISBN: 978-1-64572-099-7
ISBN (eBook): 978-1-64572-091-1

Call Me an American
Refugee to Patriot: Lessons Learned for a Strong America
© 2024 by Hung Cao with April Lakata Cao
All Rights Reserved

Cover Photo by Jim Stone Photography
Cover Design by Jim Villaflores

Republic Book Publishers
New York, NY
www.republicbookpublishers.com

Published in the United States of America
2 3 4 5 6 7 8 9 10

To my parents, Stephen and Karen Lakata, for your unconditional support. I could write a book on all the things you've done well, but it's your faith, above all else, that will impact our family's legacy for generations to come. Thank you for the way you've loved me.

To my parents, Quan and Tram Cao, for your sacrifice. You bravely embraced uncertainty to give us a new life, filled with hope. I hope that I've made you proud.

CONTENTS

FOREWORD

One of the great blessings in my life has been the opportunity to spend most of my eighty-plus years in the company of heroes. Real heroes are never selfish; they are selfless. They put themselves at risk for the benefit of others. I know. My dad was my first hero. He and all my uncles served in WWII, Korea, or both. My brothers served in combat in Vietnam and against Iranian terrorism in the Persian Gulf. They too are American Heroes. And so are the authors of *Call Me an American*—Hung Cao, and his wife, April—both dear friends, and real American Heroes.

Hung Cao's extraordinary, moving story is inspiring to anyone who loves America. He was just four years old when his parents barely escaped Vietnam, just hours before the fall of Saigon to a communist onslaught. Hung's entire family was in extreme danger. His father was targeted for assassination by the Viet Cong and the North Vietnamese Army. By the grace of God, he and his family were evacuated shortly before the South Vietnamese capital fell, and they eventually arrived in America.

In the pages ahead, you will read the powerful saga of how Hung Cao, a real refugee, came to graduate from our alma mater, the US Naval Academy, and became a deep-sea diver, a Special Operations officer, and an Explosive Ordnance Disposal (EOD) expert. During more than two decades in the US Navy, Hung Cao served in harm's way with US and allied Special Operations units in Afghanistan, the Balkans, Iraq, Somalia, and other "difficult places"—none of them locations described as "pleasant tourist destinations."

He served multiple combat tours in the Global War on Terrorism where, among many other dangerous duties, he dissected enemy Improvised Explosive Devices (IEDs) to ascertain who made them, how they made them, and how to safely dismantle them. Somehow, he also found the time, energy, and scholarly perseverance to earn an advanced degree in physics.

Years ago, I asked him, "What does it take to disarm a bomb that could kill you in an instant?"

His immediate response: "Trust in our Lord and steady hands." He wasn't joking.

Politicians and media elites pay lip service to the American dream. Few of them grasp how much Hung Cao loves America and the ways he does so! Over the years I have known Hung Cao and his family, here are just a few of the inspiring things I've heard him say when I've been in his company:

"My family and I owe everything to our Lord and the American people."

"Defending America is the greatest honor of my life."

"Serving my country in the US Navy has been my American dream."

In the pages of *Call Me an American*, Hung Cao readily admits truly believing and living the American dream. For nearly three decades, he abided by an oath to "support and defend the Constitution of the United States against all enemies, foreign and domestic..." The strength of his decisive leadership and courage against seemingly insurmountable odds in this book should motivate us all to prioritize principles over politics and cherish God-given freedom of opportunity for every American.

His life, punctuated by hardship and sacrifice, is not only a testament to perseverance but to the audacious strength that comes from faith in Father, Son, and Holy Spirit and gratitude for our Lord's gift of freedom. I stand in amazement now, much as I did when I first met him seven years ago, by Hung's story and his sheer will to overcome every obstacle standing in the way of taking care of the people he serves.

It is a privilege to call him and his wife April our dear friends. The American people are better for their service to our nation and his willingness to stand for what he believes.

Hung Cao is the most relevant person to address our present national crises. I know of no one more qualified to speak out against the socialist propaganda plaguing our military, education system, and culture. We are at a tipping point, and Hung reminds us that our power doesn't derive from bureaucrats in Washington; it's cultivated in our communities, in our homes, and around our kitchen tables.

Call Me an American isn't a book about going-along-to-get-along. Hung Cao's powerful life story makes it clear: this is not a time for equivocation or deceit in the face of divineness and chaos. This is a time for faith, integrity, and **Truth**.

"Semper Fidelis" is more than a slogan for US Marines
"Always Faithful" is a way of life

—Lt. Col. Oliver L. North USMC (Ret.)

THE DREAM ISN'T DEAD

"You're a coward." The final stinging words of a father to his son must have felt as much a promise as a curse. In the face of an impossible decision, however, the certainty of death overcame the heartbreak of disappointment. My father, a man I often struggled to understand as a young man, had already begun quietly preparing an escape from our native Vietnam. He'd hoped to leave with a blessing, free and unburdened by guilt, but in the face of abject rejection survival became a necessary motivator. Between whispered plans and unspoken fears, our charmed life in Saigon quickly faded. Through my own experiences in war and fatherhood, I see more clearly now the lens with which my parents made the decision to flee our home and country. I wonder if my mom's hand shook as she penned notes for each of us and sewed them into the hems of our clothes. Did her face reveal anxiety and doubt, or did she only reflect what I needed to see as a child; her bent over, fingers deftly guiding a needle through one more hem in quiet determination. Her steady hands and firm countenance the anchor for our family during turmoil and upheaval. Did she allow herself a moment to pause and consider the alternative to fleeing? Staying meant death or reeducation camp for my father, but leaving meant abandoning the life they built together and the people they loved. The two small suitcases she'd packed for our family of seven could not possibly hold a lifetime of memories, but it gave her the freedom to hold my hand tight as we walked away from a raging war.

Our story is not unique to the millions of immigrants who have fled war, famine, or persecution. We were one of thousands of families who escaped Vietnam with nothing but desperate hope and a desire to be free. Free from communism, free from the death and destruction that inevitably weave its ideology into the fabric of an oppressed society. In countries with authoritarian regimes, the pursuit of happiness is granted by dictate. It's not recognized as necessary for the prosperity of the human soul or the catalyst behind a thriving nation. It is intrinsically harsh, commonly destabilizing, but most importantly, conditional. There cannot be freedom when the *pursuit* is governed or mandated. Those of us who have escaped oppression recognize it for what it is: an artificial binding of the human spirit. Communism, Marxism, and socialism are the antithesis of the natural inclination of humanity to strive toward a better world, if not for us then for our own children. It deprives every man, woman, and child the opportunity to resist their own selfish nature and expound on the best of who we were created to be. Communism seeks to hem in the free thinker until the string is pulled taut enough over time to choke resistance. As a people I believe we are wild by nature. But that wildness looks different in every corner of the world. In freedom, our wild nature finds direction and purpose. We are free to aggressively pursue passions and hone talents like those that invented the airplane or sent a man to the moon. In the States, our dreams are limited only by our imagination. In contrast, oppression smothers the urge to create and innovate outside the confines of governmental dictate. It distorts incentive and demonizes wealth, placing little value on what does not benefit the collective. A strong nuclear family, great artistic talent, and scientists who test the limit of time and space have no business in a communist society unless the Communist deems it worthy for the ultimate benefit of a select few.

In the shadow of our family's American dream lives a history of tragedy and struggle. Like many refugees, our journey to freedom in the United States began long before our escape from Vietnam in 1975. The same man who called my father a coward faced his own harsh circumstances as a young man. Forced into conscription on threat of death by the Vietminh, my grandfather was ordered to join the resistance in the north. Relegated to maintaining electrical power for mobile hospitals, escape meant certain death. His expertise made him a human commodity but ensured his survival working for an enemy he loathed. My father's oldest brother was also conscripted but by the opposing French to run supplies for troops along the Laotian border. At the tender age of fifteen, my father's oldest brother was killed during a mudslide on one of his many arduous supply runs. Now, without a means of earning an income, coupled with the tragic loss of her son, my grandmother turned to alcohol for comfort. In the midst of their grief, the French, targeting their broken family as collaborators for the Vietminh, swiftly and violently destroyed their home.

Now homeless and the oldest surviving child at age thirteen, my father abandoned his education in search of a job that would support his mother and younger siblings. There was no time to grieve or consider the alternatives. The French Foreign Legion camp in Quang Tri eventually hired my father as a cleaning boy. Impressed by his stoic but amenable work ethic and intellect, a man my father called Captain Richard took notice of my father. Captain Richard was sympathetic to his plight and returned my father's work ethic with compassion and opportunity. He generously offered "Pop," as I called him, the additional task of milling rice for captured soldiers. This extra wage alone gave my father's family the opportunity to not only survive but also save for a new home. It took several years, but my father, his mother, and his three surviving siblings were able to move from an open-air, corrugated-steel-roof structure into a real home where they could finally begin to rebuild their life.

My father had much to be thankful for despite his circumstances. Captain Richard continued to be an instrumental figure in our family's story and eventually helped secure my grandfather's freedom. After years of imprisonment, with the simple stroke of a pen, my grandfather walked away from captivity and rejoined his family. His return home meant my father could once again pursue his education. After years of pouring over his younger siblings' schoolbooks in his spare time, it was his turn to invest in himself. Having developed a quiet respect for the military, thanks to Captain Richard's friendship, he'd hoped to attend the French Military School in Auxerre, France. Unfortunately, his poor eyesight quickly ended any hope of a military career. Undeterred, he earned a scholarship to the University of the Philippines through the International Cooperation Agency, the precursor to the US Agency for International Development (US AID).

By the time my parents met, they had each lived a lifetime of hardship. At the age of twelve, my mom's father was kidnapped from the courtyard outside their home. It was late in the evening, and she alone was awakened by the commotion caused by her father fighting his captors. A magistrate in the royal city of Hue, my maternal grandfather cried out to his daughter not to worry, that everything would be okay. It was the last time he was seen alive, his body never

4

recovered although his murder a certainty. That moment haunted my mom, and the consequence of his absence meant she and her siblings had to eventually be split among relatives. A former beauty queen in Hanoi, my grandmother had no way of supporting her nine children and was forced to rely on the generosity of others to sustain them.

His days of washing and scrubbing in a French Foreign Legion camp long behind him, my father was one of five students to earn the Rockefeller Scholarship for Graduate Studies at Cornell University in Ithaca, New York. It was a remarkable feat given both his broken English and broken education, but my father never succumbed to the temptation to give in to his circumstances. He proved to be resilient, adaptable, and unrepentant in his dogged pursuit of a better life. Already engaged, my mom left Vietnam to accompany him, and they were married at the Vietnamese Embassy in Washington, DC. The birth of their first child, my oldest sister, would be a thirteen-year miracle-in-waiting. Her American citizenship not only saved our family, but it paved the way for each one of us to live our own American dream.

Our current generation seems to believe the American dream is not only out of reach but also outdated. More days than not, we witness an ongoing crisis of civility along with the rewriting and retelling of history. There is a sense that this generation doesn't know what to believe about the country my family proudly and humbly calls home. It used to be that Americans wanted the opportunities of an exceptional education, home ownership, and a strong family. But there's an uneasiness that's permeated our culture, and many of us feel that the solid foundation of American pride and exceptionalism is eroding in the wake of an unwelcome cultural revolution. Technology, freedom, wealth, and comfort all play a role in this twenty-first-century pendulum swing. I find myself yearning for simpler times when truth wasn't defined by the loudest and most well-funded activist group. I don't believe the American dream is dead. It's at war with an insidious ideology desperate to erase two hundred and fifty years of progress while leading the world during the greatest times of peace, prosperity, and innovation.

According to the media, we are no longer a country united. Every day is a new revolution with Twitter trumpets announcing the latest call to action we never knew we wanted or needed. Our common values are purposefully being displaced in a coordinated effort to rid us of any sense of national pride and honor. Socialist agendas are brazenly touted in the halls of the Capitol, which always strikes me as painfully odd. I find myself laughing, not in humor but in pity, at the exhausting hypocrisy. Only in the comfort of freedom can communist ideas be expressed without life-threatening consequences. How easy it is to bemoan the very freedom protecting the speech railing against it. And at the end of the day, activists who protest our Constitutional Republic while extolling the bitterly simplistic rewards of socialism, quietly return to their homes unmolested. They sleep under a blanket of free-speech protection, virtue signals safely tucked away until the next curiously funded, well-organized protest.

I don't object to protests; in fact, I proudly served in the United States Navy as a Special Operations Officer to protect the right to do so. But I do reject the dishonest and foolhardy claim that socialism and communism are an endeavor worthy of dismantling the American dream. I reject manufactured outrage at the expense of hardworking business owners. Communist countries dominate the news cycle worldwide, a constant cataclysm of food shortages, energy crisis, and human neglect. Starving children in Venezuela, social media blackouts in Russia, families welded shut in apartments in China. All tragic examples of silent genocide under tyrannical communist rule. Pol Pot, Mao, Stalin. Vietnam, North Korea, Cuba. Generations of families extinguished under the false promise of common ownership and equitable outcomes. Yet even with the undeniable realities of communism, there are a growing number of voices, both publicly and politically, whipping the masses into a frenzy, demanding the unlimited expansion of social welfare programs, tuition forgiveness, and government-run health care. It's disturbing in its lack of honesty and obvious national consequences.

To believe socialism can prosper and not spiral into national suicide is the height of arrogance. Quite simply, it is the manifestation of a people who are restless in their freedom, uninspired by their own ability to create fruitful change within their communities. We beg government to find solutions to issues that have real, commonsense solutions at the local level if, and only if, we're brave enough to do the work. But the work is often regarded as financially prohibitive, time consuming, and void of fanfare. It takes tenacity and grit along with an intrinsic spirit of self-sacrifice to become a problem solver. Imagine if even a quarter of us recognized one need in our neighborhood and committed the time and energy to finding a solution. How quickly could food insecurity be eliminated in your town? What difference would it make to single parents for volunteers to provide free, emergency childcare or for every foster child to have a safe, secure home? It's not untenable, but are we willing to look outside our own distracted busyness and do the work? The world is filled with hashtag promises and mobilized protests, but all I see is lazy activism. In the freest country on earth resides a growing apathy in the face of perceived injustice. I marvel at the blatant lack of self-awareness. I am appalled by those who vilify liberty and hijack our history for nothing more than a chance at overnight fame and donor-funded wealth. Kneel for the flag, burn the flag but represent the red, white, and blue overseas for big money. Hate the police, burn down police stations but call 9-1-1 when triggered. Complain the American dream is dead, systemically racist, and oppressive all while creating wealth and prosperity under a capitalist system.

Maybe I see things differently because I'm an immigrant. My story did not begin with freedom, but it has ended under the Stars and Stripes with the God-given right to pursue happiness. I may not have understood my parents' sacrifice when I was young, but having left Vietnam and lived in West Africa until age twelve, I can appreciate that the contrast between them and the US wasn't just obvious, it was palpable. Freedom has its own energy. It is a current of hope that may go unspoken, but not unnoticed. For those of us who have escaped communism, economic or religious persecution, the promise of freedom was enough to risk leaving home and family. It was worth the threat of persecution and even the unfathomable risk of death. The American dream may seem to have soured for those with an ideological agenda, but for the rest of the world, and the millions of immigrants who have found a home here, the American dream is still the best chance on earth to live a life of opportunity and possibility.

When people hear my story, they often ask if I remember Vietnam or the precarious moments between escape and freedom. Not many. Most of what I remember are flashes of images instead of a steady stream of memories. What I do remember, however, are feelings. Just like freedom, fear is like a vibration. But instead of giving life, it seeps into everything around it, casting shadows on the heart and mind for years to come. When we walked away from our home in Saigon, days before the fall, my father was careful to make it appear like any other day. He had already retrieved vital documents from the embassy. He went to work as usual but gave our housekeeper the day off to visit her family. Neighbor had already begun turning on neighbor, selling reports of their suspicious activity to the enemy. We only had one chance to escape, and we couldn't risk her noticing anything out of the ordinary. My older sisters went to school, and I have no doubt my mom checked and rechecked the two small suitcases she'd packed. That day, she carefully dressed us in the clothes with money and notes secretly sewn into the hems. I now know my parents were unsure if we would be able to leave together. There was a very real fear they would have to leave one or more of us behind. I was too young to be left alone and my oldest sister was the American citizen, the sole reason we had any hope of escaping. But would any of us be allowed to go with her? Would the police stop my father, a high-ranking government official, from leaving the country or would he be captured? It was a journey of blind faith and raw hope. In the end, we made it out on one of the last flights leaving Vietnam. The journey was not easy or kind, but we were together.

Coming to the US didn't just change the trajectory of our future, it altered the legacy of our family for generations to come. My parent's sacrifice meant I wouldn't have to make the same impossible choices for my own family. When the time came, I made the decision to pay back this country for the safe refuge my family received. It's the reason I served for twenty-five years in the Navy and why I continually find ways to serve and give back in our community. It was a privilege wearing the cloth of our nation to defend life, liberty, and the pursuit of happiness. To preserve our way of life so our children can speak and worship freely. Both freedoms under direct attack over the past several years. But the American dream isn't dead. That is a lie perpetuated to convince us that we have no real power. It's a fallacy built on the premise that we are so deeply flawed as a nation that we can't possibly be good. If there is no American dream, if the pursuit of happiness is no longer the driving force or motivation for a life well lived, then we must ask ourselves why we're doing any of it. But more importantly, we must honestly and objectively consider why this narrative has gripped our country like a vice. Who ultimately benefits from it-because it's not you or me. It's not our children and certainly not their children.

Sitting on my mother's lap all those years ago, waiting for my father to join us or be lost forever, we couldn't have known what waited for us beyond those final terrifying moments. Our future was linked to our escape; there could not be one without the other. We left all our material wealth and security behind, but we never abandoned the richest currency we owned: hope. Hope is not only for the refugee or the immigrant. The American dream is not a boulevard in Beverly Hills, and it's not a privilege on loan from the government. The dream is our right to pursue happiness without compulsion or intrusion. It is for every man and woman who wakes up every day and decides they will not be defined by their circumstances. Although the pursuit does not guarantee a perfect outcome, a glass ceiling of our own making is more often our biggest barrier to success. Don't allow the rhetoric to confound you. Don't let the challenges, as formidable as they may be, stop you. My wife and I tell our kids often that nothing worth doing is ever easy. Be bold in your own pursuits because we all leave a legacy behind. Each of us must determine if that legacy is one of perseverance or one we allow to be determined by others.

As I write this, my father has been gone for ten months now. His death came as a very poignant chapter in my life closed, and a new, challenging chapter began. I wish he could have seen the joy and struggle of the past ten months. Even when November 8, 2022, ended in disappointment, it did not end the mission, and like him, I will press on in faith. I wish he could have seen the hope our message gave voters and the integrity we maintained in the face of fierce political divisiveness. Like all children, I hope he was proud of me. The campaign trail gave me the opportunity to honor his sacrifice and highlight this imperfectly beautiful nation. It gave us everything, and just as I fought to protect this country from all enemies foreign and domestic, now I fight to remind the next generation that the American dream is still worth fighting for.

THE ASSAULT ON
MERITOCRACY

t's hard being the new kid. When you're young, don't speak the language, and look different than your peers, those differences amplify the hardest parts of change. After only one year in the States, it became clear that my father's job as the Deputy Minister of Agriculture for Economic Development in Vietnam would not translate to steady work in the US. There was little opportunity in agriculture outside of farming, so when my father was offered a position as a contractor with USAID in Africa, he took it without reservation. My parents were proud people, and if living overseas meant staying off government welfare programs, that's what they would do. Once again, our family was faced with the challenge of moving to a different continent, living in a new country with a drastically different language and culture. As our plane touched down in hot, dusty Niamey, I couldn't have known what an impact that move would have on my education and beyond.

French schools were my first experience in formal education. There was no picking a seat next to new friends, no trading lunches or trinkets with a buddy for the chance to sit next to the prettiest girl in class (her name was Sandrine). The students with the highest grades sat in front while the rest sat row after row behind them according to class standing. As the new kid, small and nervous who didn't speak the language, my place in the back felt like punishment. The boys I shared the back row with were smelly and rowdy, often paddled for their antics or lack of attention. It was hard to follow along in class, and sitting next to the kids who cared the least didn't make it any easier. It wasn't a good feeling and thinking back I realize I could have allowed that feeling to defeat me, but instead it was the catalyst that motivated me to improve my circumstances.

The hierarchy and competition in the classroom did what it was supposed to do: apply passive, outside pressure to create inward change. There was no misunderstanding what was expected from students regardless of age. There was no escaping bad grades or poor performance. I wasn't allowed to hide behind my inability to speak French. I either worked my way toward the front row or accepted my fate in the back of the class. Regardless, the decision was mine and mine alone. It didn't take long, even as young as I was, to figure out that the benefits of excelling far outweighed the difficulty of learning a new language. Beginning at the elementary school level, competition was a silent partner in the learning process. Success or failure was on constant display, even in the most subtle ways. Our teachers handed out report cards by calling each student individually to the front of the room in order of merit. Performing well meant extra privileges in class or trips to the principal's office for a treat we could show off later. Students were regularly held back a grade due to poor performance. The practice wasn't meant to shame but ensured students either mastered material or had more time to mature. It took one full year of struggling, but finally sitting next to Sandrine was worth the effort.

My parents taught us that wealth or position can be taken away, but no one can take the knowledge in your head. Our life had been altered by force, but it was education that ultimately provided a path to freedom. There was nothing more important to my parents than our education, and they were relentless when it came to our studies. It was so important that by age twelve, after seven years in Africa, my parents decided my mom would return to the States with me and my two youngest sisters to learn English and receive an American education. My two oldest sisters had already left Africa one year prior to begin college in Northern Virginia, and we were to join them. The move was one more sacrifice my parents made for our benefit. My dad stayed behind in Africa for another seven years, only seeing us twice a year. His absence was a silent heartbreak and a reality that didn't sting until I was much older. It planted a quiet seed of resentment that took root and grew over the years he was gone. Even after his return home to Virginia, I kept my distance. I was a young adult too involved in my own plans, and he didn't seem to understand his Americanized son any more than I understood his sacrifice. I am thankful that God eventually found a way to dig up that root and throw it in the fire.

English as a second language is brutal. Even at fifty-one years old I prefer, and am more comfortable, speaking French. Where French is straightforward, English is filled with idioms and metaphors that sometimes confound non-native speakers. This was never more obvious to me than on the campaign trail where every word or phrase was scrutinized and dissected. As a twelve-year-old boy in sixth grade though, it was just about getting it right enough to understand I was often the butt of the joke. I was the new, scrawny Asian kid who couldn't speak English, and I was a natural target. I spent my school days in and out of English as a Second Language (ESL) classes and my spare time at home watching *The A-Team*. Hannibal and B. A. Baracus were my favorite English teachers, and it didn't take long for me to adopt my new language. By the time I was a freshman in high school, I had no accent and spoke like I'd been in the States my entire life.

In 1984, it was an exciting time in education for Northern Virginia. A new magnet school was created to attract high-performing, motivated, STEM-focused students, taking advantage of everything the proximity to Washington, DC, had to offer. Thomas Jefferson High School for Science and Technology would quickly become the number one high school in the nation, but at its conception, it was still anyone's guess how successful it would be. In my eighth-grade year, my oldest sister encouraged me to apply. The application process mirrored those of colleges nationwide with the added requirement of a rigorous entrance exam. I was resistant; it didn't seem worth the effort, but with four older sisters I basically grew up with five mothers. Trying to talk my way out of applying would have been more work than the application itself, and I grudgingly took the exam. Hindsight is a funny thing. As our experiences in life change, so does our perspective. Back then I was a kid looking to take the easy road whenever possible, but the women in my life wouldn't allow it. It's a good reminder that sometimes the best decision we make is to trust those already equipped to see the big picture. If it weren't for my sisters, I'm certain I would be in a very different place personally, professionally, and spiritually. Thomas Jefferson illuminated a path beneath my feet that carried me toward opportunity, and I will always be grateful that they saw potential in me when it was easier not to see it in myself.

We walked the halls during the initial days of our freshman year, and the hows and whys of getting there no longer seemed important. We had earned our place, rode a small wave of triumphant excitement, but the time for boasting ended as the first bell rang. Our admission had been decided by a board based on test scores and essays, and each of us bore the heavy burden of success. I was a smart kid but not brilliant. I did well enough to earn my place in the inaugural class, but I admit initially feeling out of step with my peers. I no longer spoke with an accent, but it still felt like I thought with one. English was often a mental tongue-twister, I was still small for my age, and pop culture references were often lost on me. The class of '89 collectively aspired to be doctors, scientists, and engineers, and even though I did well in math and science, they weren't my passion. I was one of few classmates who wanted to be a military officer and had my sights firmly set on the United States Naval Academy. Like all angsty teenagers, I had a long road ahead of me to discover my place and purpose among a peer group I considered intellectual giants.

We were white, black, brown, and yellow. We were kids who couldn't afford a Happy Meal and ones whose parents drove cars with fancy hood emblems. Some of us were athletes, band geeks, or the first wave of tech nerds. Many of us were refugees or first-generation Americans. We were awkward and sometimes a bit too cocky. Thomas Jefferson gave us permission to be weird because the truth was our outside didn't matter. When we crossed the threshold of TJ, we were simply defined by how hard we worked, giving us each a sense of freedom to be ourselves. One of our classmates wore overalls and a locomotive engineer's hat to school every single day. Another classmate, a Vietnamese kid like me, dressed in full punk from studded leather jacket and combat boots to spray-dyed mohawk. Some kids wore three-piece suits and carried a briefcase. The coolest guys had mullets, and the band kids wore letterman jackets with as much pride as the football team. We were all trying to carve a path for ourselves in a class of high achievers. Skin color, birthplace, and physical ability were adult problems that gained no foothold in such a highly competitive environment. Our friend with the mohawk wasn't someone to make fun of because he was brilliant and kind. It never mattered to me that I wasn't a six-foot-something white athlete. I worked out my insecurities in the classroom, the tae kwon do studio, and on my school's varsity gymnastics team. My classmates' academic achievements only pushed me to work harder and vice versa. We were the epitome of iron sharpening iron.

French school gave me a foundation in meritocracy, but TJ solidified the necessity for dogged determination. We don't always get what we want, but we certainly don't get what we aren't willing to work for. The current breakdown in education, in part, stems from a growing withdrawal from the meritocratic system of achievement. Standards have fallen right alongside expectations. The generation that got participation trophies in the nineties now hold positions of authority in education and trend toward a one-size-fits-all measurement of success. At its core, meritocracy rewards success based on individual achievement and talent, standing in stark contrast to aristocracy where wealth, socioeconomic status, and title prioritizes nepotism over individuality. It's not to say that meritocracy is perfect, but it eclipses aristocracy and has proven to be the fairest, most widely distributed measure of success. Of course, we must be aware of the reality of our human condition, which can distort opportunity through personal bias, but our charge is to remain vigilant to keep meritocracy grounded in equality.

The antithesis of meritocracy is equity. Equity is a social construct and the newest activist-driven agenda to infiltrate our cultural narrative, quickly replacing the traditional values of equality with gross subjectivity. Even our political leadership along with multibillion-dollar corporations have adopted equity as the gold standard for applying outcomes. This simple, six-letter word encapsulates the essence of communism, and its influence could not be more evident in government-run schools. Without a clear understanding of the differences between equality and equity, we run the risk of renegotiating societal norms outside the Constitution's framework for equal protection under the law. That definition of equal protection under the law defines and protects the right of all Americans to pursue opportunity without discrimination. When we talk about this type of opportunity, it doesn't mean that every person will have the opportunity to be a CEO or play in the NFL. Not many people amass tremendous wealth or fame, and not everyone can be renowned in their chosen field or profession. Equality means being fairly judged in the absence of discrimination when, and if, the opportunity presents itself.

While equality is centered in opportunity, equity is laser focused on outcomes. Where this becomes unreasonable, if not outright dangerous in a free society, is equity's unflinching ties to demographics. Ensuring an equitable outcome cannot be done without leveling the theoretical playing field in ways that stand in conflict with freedom. The push for equitable outcomes strives to eradicate factors beyond our control like economics, genetics, and intelligence, recklessly flying in the face of individuality. Quite simply, equity is manufactured discrimination promoted by the illogical rhetoric of social justice pundits. Disguised as equality, there can be no circumstance in which one or more demographic groups will not have opportunities removed from them in order to distribute or provide them to another group. Again, equity places the burden of outcomes on certain groups based on traits they can't control. Equity is a fad that will eventually cleave to the bosom of communism. It is a thief, a relic of the pre–civil rights movement resurrected by people who shot to success on the back of the very equality they claim now disparages minorities.

Not every demographic or minority group is treated equally when it comes to equitable outcomes. In fact, I have yet to hear an argument for more Asian inclusion in higher education or STEM professions. A minority group that makes up 17 percent of the population, Americans with Asian roots seem to be magically inoculated from the dire equity emergency touted by the current Administration—even when it comes to violence and public safety. My high school alma mater has been rocked by the replacement of meritocracy for a newly adopted—and questionably profitable—admission's process to force equitable outcomes. This bait and switch of choosing students in a lottery system with the intent to focus specifically on race will erode not only excellence but also trust and confidence in the education system. With parents already primed for a fight over admissions, TJ's most recent scandal may be the straw that breaks the equitable camel's back. The administration at Thomas Jefferson for Science and Technology has been accused of, and is now being investigated for, purposely withholding National Merit awards from students in keeping with Fairfax County's strategy of "equal outcomes for every student, without exception."[1] It has been suggested that this erroneous decision to withhold recognition based on the recommendation of an equity and inclusion consultant was deemed necessary to spare the feelings of students who did not qualify for the award. If true, this secret policy may have cost over one thousand students millions of dollars in scholarship money or college admission prospects. Instead of recognizing their mistake, the school board, along with administrators, continued to double down on potentially discriminatory policy. While the Commonwealth continues to investigate these claims, students remain caught in the crossfire of social justice policies, the legal system, and outraged parents. Their voice has

---

[1] Asra Q. Nomani, "Top School Principal Hides Students' Academic Awards in Name of 'Equity,'" New York Post, December 23, 2022, updated December 26, 2022, https://nypost.com/2022/12/23/top-school-principal-hides-academic-awards-in-name-of-equity.

been removed from the process even though they bear the burden of these decisions. It is their future in jeopardy, but that obvious fact is carelessly neglected by politicians who have already decided equity must be universally applied.

Equity is never about equality; it is about power. Not one sports team, from high school to the pros, chooses players based on racial demographics. Have you ever seen a five-foot-six Asian guy in the NBA? Of course not. It's about being the very best because the best sell tickets and fill stadiums. Notice how equity isn't universally applied when it affects someone else's bottom line. Denying achievement for the sake of perception is an insult to each and every person who bravely invites intellectual and physical challenges, pursuing them with fierce determination. There are no cries for equitable outcomes at the Super Bowl or the World Series. We don't ask scientists on the razor's edge of a major medical breakthrough to stop their research to allow underfunded and less equipped countries the opportunity to catch up. We use every advantage at our disposal to create miracles. When the heat stops working in the dead of winter, the search for an HVAC technician begins with five-star-rated companies, and if needed we work our way down—not the other way around. Every American should be asking serious questions about why this pervasive ideology is tolerated and how it's been allowed to change the fundamentals of education in the US. Why are adults implementing politically motivated and racially divisive policies courtesy of taxpayers at the expense of vulnerable students? If the goal is to prepare our children to handle life's challenges and become productive members of society, eliminating opportunities to fail for the sake of equal outcomes only guarantees an insecure and unreliable future workforce. In fact, most Americans believe inequality is acceptable as long as it's within a merit-based system. There's only one quarterback on the field from one team at a time. There may be others on the bench, but there is a first and best because of meritocracy. Only one valedictorian speaks at graduation, and we only elect one president.

Knowledge is the foundation of freedom and anything that seeks to manipulate or diminish its value while punishing achievement should be unapologetically scrutinized. Meritocracy works because we all naturally adhere to a primal hierarchy of success. Today, TJ has been targeted by activists who, if the same rules had been applied then, may have excluded me, or classmates like me, because we were one too many Asian students in a pile of applicants. No one wins when skin color is prioritized over test scores. Not the kids who prepared and studied to gain high marks on the entrance exam, and not the kids who didn't score as well but gained admission only to fall behind. Many of my classmates graduated and went on to become MDs, PhDs, and engineers. They've excelled in their chosen profession and beyond because they prioritized education and took advantage of every opportunity to challenge themselves. They didn't shy away from competition but used it as external motivation to push themselves beyond what they thought they could achieve. I can only imagine how many lives they have changed or affected over the past thirty years because they thrived in a meritocratic system.

Lowering the academic bar and punishing achievement is wrong. Another aspect of equal outcomes that gets too little attention is when students are accepted to colleges or magnet schools unprepared or unable to meet advanced course requirements. We do them a great disservice by setting them up for failure while also sowing seeds of distrust among their peers. When we begin questioning one another, wondering if we've been chosen because of racial demographic or competency, we mentally segregate each other. We put each other in a silent box labeled *earned* or *not earned*. Not every kid can thrive in a rigorous academic environment just like not every kid can be picked for the basketball team. We were all created with unique gifts and talents for an individual purpose, and we should collectively embrace those differences—not focus on differences we cannot change. Equity manifests artificial standards of success. I never wanted opportunity based on my race. I wanted opportunity because I earned it through hard work. Even though I didn't want to take the entrance exam for TJ, once pencil and paper were in hand, I accepted the challenge in front of me. I could handle failing, but I would have regretted not trying my absolute best. In fact, the most important lessons I've learned in life have been ones when my hard work wasn't enough. They humbled me. More importantly, they taught me to dig deep and push past the discomfort of failure.

Equity has no place in the United States. It is the fruit of a poisonous tree destined to corrupt and constrain the very best of who we are as Americans. Equity and inclusion policy thus becomes a shallow attempt at fixing a systemic problem, specifically with poor education outcomes in certain geographic areas. We have a duty and an obligation to remind the next generation that the Declaration of Independence gave us hope and a purpose for freedom that we now so easily enjoy. That framework was fought and won on the battlefield by Americans who understood that freedom and equality were worth fighting and dying for. The pursuit of happiness rests in the safety of freedom. The advancement of equity over equality, however, is a symptom of a bigger problem facing all impoverished and poor Americans that cannot be solved by quotas. My alma mater, after being ranked the number one public high school in the nation, dropped to number five within eighteen months of abandoning their tradition meritocratic admissions policy. This trend is a stark reminder that the path to hell is paved in the absence of wisdom.

Ten years ago, my father was diagnosed with bladder cancer and consequently required extensive cardiovascular workups prior to starting treatment. Treatment included surgery, and due to his age, a battery of tests was necessary to ensure his body could handle the stress of the procedure. We were all shocked when his cardiologist discovered life-threatening blockages in his coronary arteries, and my father was immediately scheduled for open-heart surgery. It was a nerve-wracking experience for all of us as we watched the patriarch of our family wheeled into the operating room. What started as a straightforward double bypass procedure turned in to a quintuple coronary artery bypass graft surgery. The road to recovery would be long, but we were incredibly grateful, even in the middle of a cancer diagnosis, that his cardiovascular disease had been discovered in time. It wasn't until later that I learned one of my father's treating physicians was my TJ classmate, Rajiv. Who would have fathomed all those years ago that Rajiv would be proof that TJ's policy to accept the most qualified students had real-world consequences. That his tenacity and drive as a teenager would later give us more time with my father. After his surgery, not only did my father live long enough to see the birth of his fourteenth grandchild and the birth of his first great-grandchild, but those eight years were a time of healing for me. That root of resentment from my youth, already withered with time and fatherhood, was replaced with the opportunity to care for him. It was finally my turn to sacrifice for him the way he had so often sacrificed for me.

FAIL FORWARD

It's not something I talk about often. I'm not ashamed of it—not now anyway—but it's not a subject that comes up organically in conversation. When I do share that part of my life, it's likely someone has come to me in crisis, unsure of how to navigate sudden failure or disappointment. Throughout my career in the United States Navy, I had the privilege of mentoring young Sailors, Soldiers, Airmen, Marines, and Coastguardsmen. Unfortunately, service members found themselves in my office on the brink of disciplinary action or at risk of being discharged altogether. Over the years I adjudicated addiction, negligence, and plain stupidity. But I also witnessed hurt, pain, and immaturity influence poor choices and actions that did not align with the military's standard of conduct. Either way, my job wasn't only to remediate but, if possible, rehabilitate. Failure has been my greatest teacher, and while it instilled in me a posture of resilience, it also served as a reminder to temper power and position with humility. Often, leadership presents an unwavering façade of perfection in order to communicate strength, but a zero-defect mentality can fracture trust. It's a fine line, especially when lives are at stake. Negotiating expectations while performing at a level of excellence can seem impossible, but the people we lead and interact with deserve the humility it requires to try. I hoped my story encouraged those suddenly facing the consequences of their actions because I was proof that redemption waits on the other side of failure. I'll never forget the day I was kicked out of the United States Naval Academy.

In 1979, my family had already lived in West Africa for several years. We were used to camels in the road and mud-hut-lined streets. During that time, turmoil in the Middle East had quickly spilled into violence, and the impact was felt internationally, especially among foreign workers. Despite the conflicts and unrest, up until that time, our life in Niger had been peaceful. My sisters rode mopeds to school, and I played with friends in a shared courtyard until the sun set. Behind a tall gate on a busy street was our modest home, right across from the French school I attended. Each evening, local men guarded the house by keeping watch outside, their presence a deterrent from petty thieves who roamed the area under the cover of darkness. As the sun receded, we could see them through the windows, swinging their swords as they talked to pass the time, pausing to observe their evening call to prayer. The dusty streets, dark skin, and foreign tongues were all I'd known, but they were the happy memories of my childhood. But when I was eight years old, my family was startled awake by pounding at our front door. It was the middle of the night, and the deep thud, thud, thud continued until my father cautiously answered. He was surprised by the presence of Marines—not the local guards—on our doorstep.

The day the Shah of Iran was deposed, Marines went door-to-door in the dark Niamey night urging Americans, and those working on behalf of the US government like my father, to seek shelter at the US Embassy for possible emergency evacuation. It felt hectic, all of us still half asleep while grabbing the few things we could carry. Our family moved quickly to join friends and neighbors, no one sure what to expect or how long we would be there. We entered the embassy under close watch and finally sheltered in place to await further instructions. I don't remember much about what we did to pass the time, but the order to remain at the embassy was short-lived and we were allowed to return home even as the Iranian government continued to be rocked by revolution. Maybe for some it would be a memory that faded with time, a moment of fear and excitement eventually forgotten. But for me, it changed everything. Those hours at the embassy shaped the trajectory of my life because of the men who loomed large over us, standing watch. Even now, if I close my eyes, I can see Marines standing at parade rest for hours at a time. Never flinching, never smiling, but always watching. It wasn't the gun at their hip but the hard, unwavering look in their eyes that filled me with both awe and peace. It said *nothing is going to hurt you tonight*. That was the first time I remember what it felt like to be safe. Within the walls of the American Embassy, I made a quiet promise to myself that I would be like those Marines: a protector. Dangerous but restrained, courageous but humble. Ten years later I fulfilled that unspoken promise by raising my right hand, swearing an oath to protect and defend the Constitution of the United States. To serve the country that offered us safe harbor and a flag to call our own. It was my turn to stand watch.

In my senior year of high school, I earned a conditional acceptance to the United States Naval Academy. Unable to get a Congressional nomination, I was sent to the Naval Academy Preparatory School (NAPS) in Newport, Rhode Island. It was a long year, one of growth, maturity, and stories to last a lifetime, but finally stepping onto the Yard in Annapolis and swearing in as a

Midshipman was truly the moment I had waited for. The class of '94 was filled with hard-chargers, and that summer we formed bonds that have lasted well over thirty years. Plebe summer was hell, but my time at NAPS and years of tae kwon do uniquely prepared me for the mental game. We couldn't wear watches and started each morning in the dark, painfully learning to gauge time by the sun in the sky and sheer exhaustion. As Plebes, we were only allowed three chews and a swallow, which meant every meal was a futile exercise in eating enough calories or not puking. Memorizing the menu for morning, afternoon, and evening meals, having current news events at the ready along with being disciplined for breathing, contributed to the constant, frantic pace of Midshipman life. Brace up, chop, square corners, chow calls, repeat, and then the academic year officially began.

Thomas Jefferson High School prepared me well, and the year at NAPS reinforced my strength in math and science. I began my Plebe year overly confident and validated several classes after taking the advice of an upper classman, hoping by my fourth year I would have done myself the favor of a lighter class load. What I didn't anticipate were the constant demands of Midshipman duties, mandatory professional knowledge, and gymnastics practice on top of a rigorous class and study schedule. By the end of my first semester, I was drowning. My academic advisor assured me every Plebe struggled during the first semester, but I would eventually find a study rhythm that fit my schedule. But it seemed inevitable that by the end of second semester, I would probably go before an academic board for remediation. I was angry at myself for not pushing back harder with my academic advisor but too filled with pride to ask for additional help. If I could just work harder, I told myself many times. Unfortunately, there wasn't enough time in the day and mine was running out. April quickly turned into May, and I joined my classmates in graduation excitement. The upper class, including my youngest sister, were preparing to join the Fleet while the Plebes anticipated, with great relief, being Plebes no more. I had convinced myself I escaped an academic board, but two days before graduation I was ordered to the Commandant's office. The Commandant, Dean of Academics, and my Company Officer were all seated behind a long green table while I nervously stood at attention. Eyes forward and chin up, I dreaded the thought of beginning my second year on academic restriction while friends enjoyed their new freedom as Youngsters beyond the Yard. But there would be no restriction. It was the Board's recommendation, based on my grades, that I be immediately separated from the Academy. I was stunned. There was no opportunity for discussion, their minds made up long before I submitted myself before the Board. My only recourse was to appeal the decision to the Superintendent within twenty-four hours. The appeal was denied immediately and unceremoniously. My final duty as a Midshipman was to turn in my gear and leave school grounds. I don't have a clear memory of that day, each moment hazier than the next as the reality of my consequences sank in. I could not see past my failure or conceive of a way forward because there was nothing else I wanted to do and no one else I wanted to be. My dream, along with my identity, died in that office, and I was devastated.

I went to my room and sat in silence with the lights off, unable to face the shame of calling my parents. I had tried and failed. I had prioritized the wrong things instead of admitting I couldn't do it all. I should have advocated for myself instead of hoping things would get easier. Now, many years later when I think of that moment, I cringe because the memory of those feelings is so uncomfortable. I was broken and terrified, utterly ashamed of myself. A second-year student found me in my room and offered his encouragement, reminding me that at the very least, the school couldn't stop me from reapplying. I don't think he meant it to be taken as advice, but I wasted no time and sought out the Dean of Admissions and asked him if readmission was possible. *Technically*, he said, *anyone could reapply after one year but would have to demonstrate a compelling reason for readmission.* He made it quite clear, gently so I would come to the obvious conclusion on my own, that only 10 percent of total new applicants were admitted per year. The chance of accepting a repeat student with a tarnished academic record was highly unlikely. The dismissal did not preclude me from reapplying, but I would be better served moving on and taking another path. His answer was more a kindness than reality, but in my daze all I could hear was hope. A day later, my sister graduated. I sat in the stands with my family, no longer in uniform but civilian clothes, pretending I wouldn't rather be anywhere else and hating myself for not celebrating her achievement. The excitement was palpable, the atmosphere one of celebration and reverence. At the end of the ceremony covers were tossed high in the air with a collective shout of joy, signifying the beginning of their new journey and the abrupt end of mine. While my friends and classmates put on new shoulder boards to mark the conclusion of Plebe year, I was reeling on the inside. I had no path forward and nothing but humiliation to show for the past two years. Maybe I'd never carried that dream out of Africa, after all.

Imagine the risks we wouldn't take if we knew we were destined to fail. We would tread so lightly through life we'd never leave footprints deep enough for others to follow. Those of us who have walked this journey know the first instinct after failure is to quit. The fear of failure, conceived in disappointment and rooted in inaction, can be overwhelming, but it doesn't have to define what we do next. Over the past hundred years, incredible feats of human achievement and technological advancement have captivated generations of Americans. To our detriment, we aren't always privy to the sacrifice and struggle that birth perseverance on the long and rocky road to success. I am extraordinarily grateful for the people who didn't shrink away in my moment of failure, who didn't treat me like the shame would rub off by association. They offered wisdom and guidance—even unknowingly—not in a false attempt to excuse my mistakes, but to push me past my own perception of reality. So often the choices we make in the days after failure can determine our future success. When faced with defeat, it's easy to allow bitterness or self-pity to become the scaffolding we hang our personal narratives on. Excuses and deflection don't just become a downward spiral but a wall we erect to keep us from necessary, and sometimes painful, introspection. That wall, coupled with society's notion that our circumstances have more to do with outcomes than our individual behavior, can solidify a victimhood mentality. How easy it would have been to disparage my teachers or leadership. How simple it is, and how much better it can feel, to blame those who advise us when the result is not victory. There is a time to mourn loss, of course, but we have a greater responsibility to reject the narrative of victimization and push forward—even if it means clawing out of the proverbial pit to do so.

There was no way that Youngster could've known his off-handed remark sparked a nineteen-month journey to earn reacceptance to the Naval Academy. Maybe on the outside it seemed like the desperate actions of a young man who couldn't face the reality of his mistakes, but it was the push I needed to regroup and refocus. Moving forward while managing my family's expectations wasn't easy, though. They were embarrassed I'd been kicked out and could not understand why I would expose myself to further rejection. For them, the only thing left to do was what I should have done in the first place, become an engineer. Do what was safe and expected. Forget the military (my mom had hated the idea from the beginning) and do what was right as the only boy in our family. I knew they were disappointed, and I hated that I'd let them down more than I cared to admit, but I still believed the Academy was where I belonged. I immediately enrolled in our local university as a guest matriculate for the summer, supplementing my studies at the community college until I was accepted as a full-time student in the fall. Come spring, I was accepted to the School of Electrical and Computer Engineering. Buoyed by a 3.8 GPA and intense class schedule, I meticulously prepared my admission's package for the Academy, determined I had demonstrated a renewed dedication to my studies. That confidence was shattered, however, when a thin white envelope arrived several weeks later.

The road to redemption was long, and at nineteen I was not particularly good at waiting so keeping myself busy became a priority. When I wasn't at school or studying, I was helping a longtime friend open a karate studio. Both of us had been dedicated students of Jhoon Rhee, often called, "the father of American tae kwon do," and I spent every spare minute teaching while my friend built his business. Grandmaster Rhee hadn't just been a Master of tae kwon do but a master in humanity. He had a gift for understanding what motivated people and delighted in teaching us to take ownership of our outcomes; to own both our successes and failures. And fail we did. When I was fifteen, I did not pass my second-degree black belt test, and it took me a year to gain the courage to retest. Master Rhee was tough, but he was fair. He didn't fill us with a false sense of entitlement, but neither did he condemn us when we fell short of his expectations. An immigrant to the US in the 1960s, Jhoon Rhee was profoundly patriotic, teaching us to combine passion and purpose for the benefit of others. He was strict, unwavering in his principles for life while exemplifying American values. His guidance and firm hand had been exactly what I needed as a kid growing up with a father living overseas. After I was dismissed from the Academy, teaching allowed me to hone my leadership skills, but more importantly, it gave me a reason to get out of my own head and focus my attention on the people around me. Many of my students came from broken homes or were doing poorly in school. We partnered with worried parents and helped rambunctious boys channel their energy. I instructed my students to build on their strengths and honestly address weaknesses, which helped reinforce my own need to be patient during growth. I was using this same formula to quietly deconstruct my own life, especially on the heels of my second rejection letter from the Academy.

One of my student's parents was a military officer who expressed appreciation for the discipline I had instilled in their child. Only one of few to know my intention to reenter the Naval Academy, he graciously offered me the opportunity to sit down with his boss, a Major General, in the hopes I would receive wise counsel and guidance for the future. With a second rejection letter already in hand, there was mounting pressure from both friends and family to move on. And although I was doubting the wisdom of reapplying for a third time, I could not ignore the voice encouraging me to keep going. Although I know now it was God, at the time all I had was enough faith in that voice and the feeling that it wasn't over. I met with the Major General and he interviewed me for over an hour about my life and intentions for the future. When the meeting concluded, he surprised me by offering to write a personal letter of recommendation to the Superintendent of the Naval Academy on my behalf. It was extraordinarily generous. To my surprise, I received a call one month later from the admissions office asking me to report to the Academy to interview with four Department Heads: three Navy Captains and a Marine Colonel. For what purpose I couldn't be sure, and they certainly didn't offer any more information other than a report time and location. It was October, the academic year already well underway; I watched Midshipmen bustle to and from class as I waited for my first meeting. I wasted no time acknowledging my missteps during my Plebe year. I was honest about where I'd gone wrong but confident in where I wanted to go. Sixteen months had taught me that my failure wasn't a character flaw, and I didn't want it to become the most important part of my story. I was finally learning that growth and perseverance were best experienced on the other side of adversity, making me a better candidate than I'd been the first time. I left all four meetings unsure of the impact I'd made but thankful for the chance to be heard. Regardless of the outcome, I knew I'd been given an opportunity that doesn't often come that early in life. It was the endurance to finish what I'd started even if it meant an end to that part of my dream. Even if the outcome was not readmission, I was still committed to finding another way forward. I pulled away from Annapolis with renewed excitement and a surprising sense of peace.

The next several months were quiet, although I was curious why I'd been asked to meet with senior officers only to hear nothing further. I chalked it up to the school's due diligence before finally sending me an official *stop applying, it's never going to happen* letter. Life was busy with classes, martial arts tournaments, and teaching, and I finally stopped holding my breath when I checked the mail. On January 2 I happened to be spending a rare afternoon at home. When the phone rang, I answered absentmindedly, my thoughts elsewhere. A woman asked for me by name, which I nervously acknowledged. She laughed and said with a hint of surprise, *Congratulations, you're the one—the only one. Pack your things and report in the morning.* And then she hung up, and I was left to stare confused at the phone. How could this happen in the middle of an academic year? There hadn't been time to ask questions or make sure I heard her correctly. I can laugh about it now, but in all honestly, even though I knew reapplication was possible, I hadn't ever heard of anyone being readmitted. No one had. Now it had happened, and I was stunned, having less than twenty-four hours to report to Annapolis. The next morning, I was sworn in by the

Deputy Commandant, officially joining the class of '96. My former classmates were now senior to me, reminding me that I was a Plebe again, and my new classmates were complete strangers. I was suddenly reliving the hardest year at the Academy, and I couldn't have been happier.

We all fail. It's the worst and best part of life, even if we can't see it in the moment. But the failing should not be the end of our journey. If we allow it, strength comes when we're stretched and pulled beyond what we think we can handle. Too often I see young people celebrating failure like it's a badge of honor. Our culture is in sincere danger of forgetting that it's not the falling down but rather the getting back up that instills the resilience we need to navigate life well. Our country needs men and women who are willing to strive for excellence, seeing potential beyond the fear of failure in order to create lasting change in our communities. We must make peace with the reality that failure teaches us to be brave while steadily increasing our resolve in the face of adversity. My parents demonstrated perseverance, but they could not save me from the inevitability of failure. I had to be allowed to fail in my own way to finally grow into the man I believe God and my country needed me to be. Most importantly, we have an obligation to allow our children to fail early and often, supporting them—but not fixing it—as they experience the repercussions of failure for themselves. Negotiating risk and experiencing consequences in a supportive environment will fortify them for adulthood and strengthen the next generation of Americans.

During the 2022 midterm election, I liked to tell a story on the campaign trail about why failure and adversity are essential to a strong, cohesive society. In the 1980s, a biodome was erected in the desert in Arizona to replicate a perfect, artificial living environment. Every detail was controlled from the air, the water, and the light; each species of plant and tree having exactly what it needed to survive and thrive. But scientists were baffled when trees, seemingly for no reason, fell over when they reached a crucial point of maturity. Mysteriously, healthy trees could not sustain their own height despite being grown in a uniquely protected environment. In the end, scientists had simply overlooked one vital component: adversity. They hadn't considered that storms, even ones that threaten to splinter or uproot, are vital for growth. When strong, gusty winds cause a tree to bow and bend, it forces their roots to advance deeper into the soil to provide strength and stability. And depending how we choose to live our lives, we are either like the trees in the biodome or the ones standing tall after the storm. Controlling our circumstances or avoiding adversity in the name of self-preservation may feel better in the moment, but eventually it weakens our ability to survive and thrive after life's most challenging trials. Conversely, taking risks out of obedience and faith, even if we fail, strengthens and steadies us for the next opportunity to succeed. And there will always be other opportunities; we must only be ready when they come. I haven't regretted a single moment since getting kicked out of the Academy. In fact, I always tell people whom I share this particular story with that I had to leave the Academy to find God and my wife. Because without both, I would not be who I am today.

In the early morning hours at the embassy in West Africa, the Marines weren't a fairytale or characters in dress-up clothes. They were real men who'd no doubt already experienced personal challenges and disappointments in their young lives. Yet they still stood on that wall, embodying a spirit of excellence and dedication that resonated so deeply with this little Asian kid that it followed me all the way into adulthood and my own naval career. They didn't allow anything, not their past mistakes or future failures, to get in the way of their duty that night, and they were exactly the kind of men I wanted to be. The day I finally threw my cover in the air on graduation day, I knew I was one step closer to fulfilling that dream. I had failed, but I did not quit. The world doesn't need everyone to be a Marine, Soldier, or Sailor. But what it does need are people mentally strong enough to see failure as an opportunity to reprioritize and strengthen their resolve. I've seen too many men and women give up after they fail the very first time. That tells me is that it wasn't as important to them as they believed because it can't be enough to quit when it feels bad. There must first be a good-enough reason not to continue before choosing to go in a different direction. Oftentimes the road we've chosen isn't the right one, but that's okay too. In that case, we have to depend on wisdom and clarity to discern the lesson from the process, not the dream itself. Don't overlook or dismiss the lessons learned during the process; that is a success in its own right. Failure can also be an opportunity to distinguish a passion from a vocation. Not every passion is meant to support a family even if it gives us the greatest joy, and not every vocation fills us with complete satisfaction even though it provides for our family. The balance comes when we recognize and prioritize our primary purpose, never being afraid to try and fail. My encouragement during these times is simple. When you wake up in the morning, wondering if you're on the right path or if you should try again, ask yourself this one question: *Who am I standing watch for today?* The answer may surprise you.

A DEEP DIVE
ON DIVERSITY

We were at a Wardroom function when we heard the news. A Piper 32 down in Martha's Vineyard with American political royalty missing. Once again, the Kennedys captivated the nation as tragedy unfolded on CNN. The sudden shift from sea stories to mission planning ushered in a sense of calm urgency. Those first sparks of adrenaline, when the switch flips and the training and experience settle in, this is when the good stuff happens. Within thirty minutes we had nautical charts from the ship rolled out on the dining room table, beer cans pushed aside, and the food long forgotten while our wives prepared for us to be gone. A downed aircraft required salvage and recovery, and the call we knew was imminent meant getting underway with little notice under intense public scrutiny. The wide expanse of the Atlantic Ocean was shown on a loop as commentators speculated, but as deep-sea divers, we knew our focus most likely rested some-where on the bottom of the ocean. While news anchors peddled possibilities, the sobering reality of an ocean recovery and all that it entailed had us speaking in hushed voices. Death is the great equal-izer. It doesn't matter if you are rich or poor. There is no special dispensation for being the son of a president any more than being the daughter of a mechanic. Everyone who has ever lived will have an end; the only difference is the how and when.

I was barely two years out of dive school and eighteen months onboard the USS *Grasp* when tasked to coordinate the search efforts for John F. Kennedy Jr. his wife, Carolyn Bessette- Kennedy, and his sister-in-law, Lauren Bessette. I was young, untested, and third in command, and the mission included multiple state and federal agencies along miles of ocean. The ship had recently under-gone a scheduled turnover, and the new crew considered me a more seasoned diver and officer among our small Wardroom. That assumption couldn't have been further from the truth. As we pulled away from the pier in Norfolk, the scope and size of what awaited us gave me pause. It wasn't that I was afraid; in fact the opposite was true. All operators welcome the opportunity to use the skills we've developed with blood, sweat, and tears. But the ache after a training exercise is nothing compared to the mental and physical exhaustion after a mission. The training creates muscle memory meant to desensitize; to override and replace our intrinsic fight or flight response. The aftermath of a mission lingers while the sights, sounds, and smells live in the recesses of the mind. Fear wasn't my companion as we made our way north. It was failing the families, the crew, and myself that I wrestled with in those first few hours at sea. Divers I'd hoped would teach me to navigate the intricacies of running a large, joint-recovery operation—quiet warriors who played a key role in the tragic recovery of TWA Flight 800—had long gone, taking with them their wisdom and demons. In the days to come, however, the confidence of the Captain and the professionalism of the crew anchored me as we worked with little sleep and strict dive timetables that constantly threatened our search capacity. When I look back now, I see the ways this changed me professionally and prepared my mind for the years of war to come.

When the *Grasp* arrived in Martha's Vineyard, searchers had been in the vicinity for three days yet had failed to locate the missing plane. The urgency to find the crash location was heightened by constantly shifting currents and the very real possibility of losing the wreckage before it was ever found. Once on-station, our Captain took tactical control of the search efforts with an understanding that this was no longer a rescue operation. Commanding Officers from each of the twelve search vessels including the Coast Guard, NOAA (National Oceanic and Atmospheric Administration), the Massachusetts State Police, along with other Navy ships, convened onboard where I briefed our plan to impose a new, methodical grid search. We would deploy divers only after verifying reliable sonar contacts, sweeping up and down the grid based on the final transmission from the single-engine aircraft. After the meeting, I took my place on the bridge to direct assets while filtering incoming communication traffic from the influx of side-scan and towed-array sonar findings. Divers were splashed in the water with each new credible echo, the search area continuing to shrink until finally, less than twenty-four hours after the *Grasp*'s arrival, we found the missing plane and her passengers. At one hundred and twenty feet, in the cold waters off Martha's Vineyard, the first part our mission ended as murky underwater footage revealed the crushed wreckage. For everyone intimately involved in the recovery phase, it would prove to be the most challenging. Not because the world was watching, but because, up until then, the families had delayed their grief until we broke the surface and their hope.

I wasn't supposed to dive during the recovery phase. When the Chief Petty Officer appeared on the bridge I was surprised, my attention divided between operations taking place on and off the ship. He informed me I was one of only two clean divers left out of twenty and the Captain wanted the plane recovered without delay. The brief was quick, the mission to rig and retrieve the plane completely intact on the first attempt not a suggestion. I had one chance to get it right. As the stage lifted up and over the deck, my gloved hands gripped the rail in front of me. I took a few even breaths as the cold ocean water crept through my wetsuit, up my legs, torso, and finally covered my head. On the bottom, our progress toward the wreckage was painfully slow as clouds of silt obstructed our view. With each step forward I paused, letting the silt settle before putting the other foot forward until, finally, what had once been a plane came into view. At the bottom of the ocean, silence amplifies destruction. When you can only hear yourself exhale, heartbeat pounding in your ears, there is no distraction from the reality of what your eyes see and hands feel. You remind yourself you're doing a job and the rest can wait until you close your eyes at night. Our first task was to confirm the bodies were appropriately secured in the basket. After communicating with the ship, we watched them ascend, knowing their families would be waiting. Next, we began securing lines around the twisted metal in a way we hoped would allow it to be hoisted to the top without fracturing. Every edge seemed jagged or frayed. It was like securing a rope around a metal can that had been stomped on by a heavy boot. We had one shot to ensure the integrity of the plane, knowing an investigative team waited on the surface. Before the plane could be recovered, the other diver and I made our way to the dive platform and began our own ascent. We had to be clear of the plane in case the lines snapped and it plunged back into the ocean. Miraculously, the plane was pulled to the surface in one piece. The family, including

Senator Ted Kennedy, came onboard to pay their respects to the crew for their hard work and dedication over the last several days. When they finally took their final steps off the ship, I think we all breathed a collective sigh of relief. Our part of the mission was over, and we'd given the family the very best of ourselves. I looked out over the ocean, ships anchored and helicopters flying overhead, and felt completely spent with exhaustion and gratitude. I watched as the Sailors busied themselves, already preparing to get underway and return home. I took a deep breath of ocean air tinged with the smell of diesel and returned to the bridge. The final stage of our journey meant a few more sleepless nights and then we'd be home.

My first operation behind me, what I continued to learn during my time onboard the *Grasp* would serve me throughout my twenty-five-year career. Not only was I exposed to challenging circumstances, but I was also exposed to challenging people. Conflict was normal but so was resolution. Even as a pre-9/11 military, readiness overcame egos and personality. We learned to embrace the suck for the sake of the mission ahead, fortifying ourselves with thick skin through lessons learned. I believe the military, for all its flaws, represents the best of who we are as Americans. I don't think there's any other industry in the country that compares to the diverse talent found in the United States Armed Forces. From engineers to doctors, to technicians and war fighters, every specialty returns to the core mission of either defending our national security or supporting those who do. Despite boasting service members of all ages, races, and backgrounds, the military remains cohesive because the vast majority of us live by the same code: to protect and defend the greatest nation on earth.

We understood the importance of the collective in order to preserve the individual; COVID tainted this ideology, and we are, unfortunately, living with the repercussions of our government's gross overstep. At the heart of who we were in uniform, we were

Americans first. Everything else was secondary. It didn't mean we forget or ignored who we were; in fact, our lives and experiences brought immeasurable value to the job. It meant we prioritized our duty over the need to aggressively stand out in the way we're experiencing in society. Now, the value of individuality has shifted from freedom and autonomy to a hyper-focused, forced recognition of race and sex. In the military we emphasized adapting to the people and circumstances around us, but it was always for the good of the mission. Now, we're all expected to adapt to race and gender ideology not for the good of the nation, but for the good of select social agendas. Nowhere is this more relevant than the aggressive, oftentimes nonsensical talking points surrounding the diversity, equity, and inclusion (DEI) agenda.

The devolution over the past several years has been staggering. We seem to be advancing the same destructive framework of Jim Crow but this time with slick rebranding to promote selective segregation and equity. It's been hard to watch, and I feel confident speaking for most Americans when I say that defining each other by qualities that are unchangeable, like skin color, will only lead to an accepted dehumanization of specific classes of people. If skin color is the primary attribute by which we judge worth, then what does it say about who we are as a nation? All I see is a movement trying to resurrect the same twisted sentiment pervasive during slavery and before the civil rights movement in order to further a progressive agenda. There is no shortage of examples how the logic of relating every facet of a civilized society to skin color only breeds resentment, divisiveness, and chaos. The cult of diversity, equity, and inclusion has led to segregated college graduations and medical schools willfully implementing "separate but equal" spaces. Sound familiar? It does and it's appalling. Our finest institutions for science and medicine are leading the charge to indoctrinate a generation of health-care providers to see skin color and race before the humanity of their patients. What I see in our future is the prioritization of health care based on skin color or race. If we continue to push a narrative with the sole purpose of demonizing and mischaracterizing one race of people in order to elevate another, we are already in a fight for the soul of our nation. We've been here before, and it's interesting how the same political party was the catalyst for the justification of segregation both then and now. It's tragic because thousands of men died on the battlefields of their brothers to break the chains of racism. In 1963, men and women of all colors linked arms and marched on Washington to end inequality and segregation, yet separate spaces for certain races are now becoming commonplace despite a civil rights movement that changed the landscape of American history for the better. Race relations in the United States aren't at a standstill; we've actually done a U-turn on the altar of diversity and inclusion.

What we bear witness to today is not a push for diversity. At least not diversity of experience or thought in a way that supports and encourages ingenuity and advancement for the betterment of the country and mankind as a whole. What we're living through again is the elitist experiment of elevating skin color and race as the highest example of moral authority. And it's been easy. The information superhighway is their bullhorn, and it's been an effective tool to capitalize on the ruination of men and women who share any difference of opinion counter to what the elite believe, especially in academia. The playbook is not new, but the manner in which accusations of racism or bigotry are promulgated have had devastating consequences in an incredibly short amount of time. When the mob has access to personal and professional information, primarily via social media, the mob quickly learned that they could dictate compliance. And so they did. They recognized how jarring it was to the human spirit to be publicly accused of bigotry, and that single realization is being exploited and capitalized on in the most grotesque ways. We see a generation of people paralyzed by the financial or social consequences of speaking out against policies that threaten the well-being of our children and communities. The DEI mob knows that if they can ruin reputations, they will maintain control of the narrative. Diversity, equity, and inclusion policy was never designed to encourage people from different backgrounds, education, and experiences to work toward a common goal. It was never about promoting the best and brightest. Do not be fooled into believing this special brand of inclusivity can be anything other than exclusive. With DEI, the threshold for success is based solely on external identifiers independent of the long-term ramification of policies that themselves prove to be explicitly discriminatory. Colleges and corporations now boast of their own virtue in order to gain social credit alongside well-funded, disproportionately loud special interest groups who have turned our litigious society into a power scheme meant to force dissenting voices into silence.

This chapter isn't for people who believe that diversity, equity, and inclusion belong in our schools, military, sports, and corporations. If you can't understand why discrimination based on race or skin color is wrong, then that is a problem that cannot be solved in one chapter of a book. Yours is a heart issue. What I will offer is a reminder that skin color is not an accomplishment. It doesn't make someone better or worse, privileged or oppressed, weak or strong. I should not be given special accommodations or access because my skin is brown. I have never wanted a job I wasn't qualified for, and I certainly never felt entitled to take it from someone who has lighter skin than me. Like many before me, I have experienced discrimination from childhood through adulthood. If you allow it, it can defeat you, warping your perspective. Instead of using the precious time and energy it took to complain, I worked so hard that the arbiters of that discrimination had no choice but to yield to my knowledge and skill set. The presupposition of men makes no difference to me. I choose how I am defined, and I believe it is through honor, integrity, and service. If you see skin color first and make an initial assumption about an individual based on outward appearance, I contend you are the problem. In fact, I would argue that you are no different than the people who lived a quiet, safe life while one group of people were relegated to the back of the bus. You are raising kids who will grow up to be what you claim you hate because you're teaching them to judge a person's outside first and foremost. Stand for who you believe are the oppressed and the vulnerable but be honest about your motivations. Are you making a political statement, or do you want to change the world? The people who do the real work don't do it behind a computer screen or in the streets with prefabricated signs and matching T-shirts. They sacrifice their time and energy and go into communities that are hurting. They teach kids to read, become a mentor, and volunteer at shelters. They crochet blankets for the homeless, organize a food drive, or hold the hand of a pregnant teenager in complete anonymity. They don't care about skin color; they care about people and haven't allowed political or social bias to erase individuality. They put on their hard hat, jump in the ocean, and submerge themselves in the heartbreaking, beautiful work of humanity.

Skin color should never have been a disadvantage and should not be an advantage now. It cannot predict intelligence or outcomes, and it certainly does not dictate one's individual moral compass. Yet we now attribute a person's most superior qualities with the amount of melanin in their skin over honesty, integrity, loyalty, or generosity. When diversity inclusion policy became a marketable product, we began forfeiting our humanity on the altar of equity. Does racism exist? Sadly, yes. A racist is the first to boast of his own bigotry. People can be cruel and evil, and that will not end while humans roam the earth. But a race war has been waged for power with national division a gleeful by-product for those who profit. They know we are stronger united, but it does not fit their agenda to fundamentally transform this country, and so they persist. We have an obligation and a duty to reject the DEI agenda because at its core it seeks to destroy and divide people into haves and have-nots. It legitimizes discrimination and promotes victimhood, while threatening to erase the prevailing values of hard work and perseverance. If we continue down this path, we must consider how far we're willing to go. Who decides what is diverse, inclusive, or equitable enough? I contend we'll become so myopic in our quest for equitable outcomes, we will lose our position as a superpower when the scales are precariously tipping toward a world war. We're already well on our way given our current economic decline and failures in military recruitment. We've begun quietly handing over our sovereignty to elite globalists who push Marxist policies like DEI from their guarded homes and private jets. Let's not be fooled that those who rail against the supposed inequitable, systemic racism in America really believe their own drivel. Everyone can see, if there is any desire for truth over ideology, that these same people have wealth and success due to the freedom they exploit yet hope to crucify. The hypocrisy would be laughable if it hadn't had such a negative and divisive effect on our country.

I learned an interesting lesson when I ran for Congress during the 2022 midterm election. At the height of the primary, those on the Left liked to point out that their party was spectacularly diverse while the Republican party only boasted old white men. It's not historically inaccurate, but over the years there has been a noticeable uptick in the number of conservative minorities serving in elected office from the local to federal level. The reasons for this are for another time, but expect the trend to increase as socialist policies and rampant illegal immigration are perpetuated by progressives within our own government. Our district is mostly blue, and we knew it would be an uphill battle, but I appreciated the fight it would take to gain ground and win. After all, we live in Loudoun County, the wealthiest county in the country, where an above-average number of adults hold degrees in higher education. I looked forward to robust debates and honest conversations with people who think differently than me. If there was ever a place where I thought honest, intellectual discourse would serve as a beacon of hope for our community and state, this would be it. I couldn't have been more wrong. Here I was, a war refugee to this country with a decorated military career, a master's degree in physics, fellowships from Massachusetts Institute of Technology and Harvard, with an extensive background in national security and budgeting, and there were very few who wanted to engage. I was astonished by the lack of intellectual curiosity. At a time of record inflation, a floundering GDP, middle-class families suffering under the weight of high gas and food prices, along with record drug overdose deaths in young adults, I looked forward to offering solutions to move our country forward.

It was during the beginning of the second debate I realized a very large population of people do not want true diversity. In fact, they don't want anyone who looks or thinks differently than them, which is quite incongruent with their social justice activism. Their social media profile pictures are flags and hashtags, but their actions paint a picture of exactly who they are when you won't conform to their ideology. It was clear the women in the audience didn't want to understand why someone who looks like me believes in the principles of life, liberty, and the pursuit of happiness. They were there not as participants in the political process but as a tool of the Left to ridicule and mock to make their point. This is what they do when the facts are not on their side. Sitting at a table in front of constituents, those opposing my campaign displayed their contempt in the most juvenile manner. I shared my story of being a war refugee, the gift of US citizenship, and the opportunity our family was given after we lost our home, language, and culture. I spoke of being a veteran and believing in sacrifice over self-interest, duty instead of power. I was a man who grew up in a predominantly black, Muslim nation, raised Buddhist, and took advantage of every opportunity freedom in the United States gave me. Instead of considering a perspective birthed from both diversity and adversity, even on points of disagreement, row after row of women patiently waited. As the first word left my mouth, each raised their white palms with fingers spread wide so I could see the words "liar" and "asshole" clearly written on them. When my opponent accused me of not caring about babies outside the womb—an illogical and deeply flawed talking point used by pro-abortion activists at nauseum—I shared our family's journey of adoption. They laughed. I was already used to the outlandish rhetoric my opponent used to deflect from her abysmal voting record. Her favorite monikers: extremist, bigot, and MAGA Republican were tools right out of a tired, repetitious playbook to inflame and stoke fear in voters. This new approach, however, the venomous audacity, was truly disheartening when put in context of the future of our children. These women are mothers, daughters, and wives, and their answer to opposing moral viewpoints and policy differences was to scribble profanity on their hands. I was embarrassed for them. They hold influence in their professions and are responsible for the next generation of leaders in this country, yet this is what they resorted to in their rabid pursuit of diversity and equity. They were so blinded by hate they couldn't even see how their own party used them as pawns in a petty game. Their fundamental idea of tolerance is a cult of willful ignorance. Their hostility only affirmed why—after years of military service, when a quiet life would have been easier—I entered the race for a different kind of public service. It's because we desperately need a return to civil discourse. It's important to be reminded that tolerance becomes sacrificial when our ideals rub up against conflicting viewpoints. It takes strength of character to consider the experiences and opinions of others and weigh them against our own worldview without a disrespectful, emotional response. That is the true meaning of diversity and inclusion. This is what tolerance should look like, but all I saw were women who used their voice to become the exact model of what they claimed to hate.

Like the women at the debate, too many of our fellow Americans have lost their perspective. There has been too little sacrifice and too much entitlement. From those of us who have spent a lifetime serving in silence, there has been too little resistance. While many of us pushed ourselves to the brink mentally and physically on foreign soil, an insidious ideology of divisiveness flourished at home. Instead of seeking common ground, at all costs looking for ways to come to the table in agreement for the good of all Americans, corrupting powers persevered over people. We name-call, virtue-signal, and point out skin color to further a narrative that does not support facts or common sense. We have ignored violence while espousing violence in order to justify violence all in the name of equity. Diversity isn't the goal, inclusion is inherently subjective, and equity will dismantle society until there are only the very rich and the very poor. I contend that in the end, what we leave behind for our children and grandchildren will be determined by our experiences and how we chose to treat the people around us. I have lived and seen enough of the world to give me a clear perspective that values life and liberty above political ideology, rendering their shallow attacks impotent. It doesn't change the truth. We are Americans first, dedicated to the principles that made our country free, and no one has the right to dictate our language to fit their distorted perception of what this country should be. The time has come and gone for us to sit quietly on our hands, hoping someone will finally come along and change the reality that we are a nation in decline. We will be unrecognizable if we continue down this path, segregating ourselves to the point that we refuse to even identify as Americans. We will be a country unmoored from our founding, a wreckage of our former selves as a consequence of multiple generations indoctrinated in diversity, equity, and inclusion policy. What we're witnessing now is not a result of the past three years, but gradual changes in both education and culture over several decades. Only now is it being exposed for its insidious influence on society.

We must harness the lessons from our past in order to ensure a strong future. I learned from men who had tattooed knuckles and were weathered and worn by years at sea. Salty Chiefs who swore and drank but showed up before the sun rose and left long after their men went home. Admirals who modeled excellence and showed me that power is a burden and to respect the ways it can ruin you. I never let the naysayers intimidate me. Not my classmate at the Academy—furious that I'd been selected over him as one of six Midshipmen for the Special Operations community—who got me in a room alone just to tell me how worthless I was. Not the politicians who slander and lie for a living. Not even the people I thought loved me and my family but abandoned us over politics. We must refuse to be intimidated. Although the last several years have been difficult, I don't believe the worst days are behind us. But I do believe we are on the cusp of a national revival *if* our voice is louder than those counting on their divisive rhetoric to fuel their agenda. The Left has clearly defined a strategy to shape and manipulate the narrative. They've learned, adapted, and overcome meek pushback while blazing a destructive, but effective, trail forward. They counted on us staying silent, of being too afraid of offending or being called names. And we were, and they did anyway. While we were practicing tolerance for the sake of the culture, they were pushing us into a cultural corner. They waged a war of words, and we must be willing to do the same, but our commitment must always be to the truth. The first step is to stop ignoring the outlandish lies we hear daily. Call them out for what they are but be ready with facts and not feelings. We are not a racist nation. Parents, not teachers' unions, have a fundamental right to know what is happening in their kids' schools. The color of your skin does not define you. Tolerance is not love if it perpetuates a lie. Race does not make you the better person for the job. True diversity begins in the mind, and it's our experiences that bring value to our work and communities. Use the lessons in your life to relate to the people around you instead of talking points. Our job isn't to convince people they're wrong, but to be involved to the point they can't ignore the good. That's what wins hearts and minds and destroys narratives. It's hard for the neighbor who is fed and comforted by you to believe you're a threat to democracy. The false elevation of race and gender can't thrive when everyone is working toward the same goal.

It's time for a national shift, a revival centered in hard work and individual exceptionalism to combat the purposeful dismantling of our identity as free-thinking people. But it won't work if each of us believes the solution lies in the next person. Don't expect anyone to change what you are unwilling to confront or fight for in your own life. We all have the power and strength to make a difference, each of us a pebble in the pond causing that first small ripple. Eventually, if enough people stand for American values and against the current DEI agenda, that pebble becomes a stone creating waves strong enough to effect change. That is how the tide finally turns. Stand for truth and don't compromise out of fear because there will come a day when it is too late. You must only look at how easily our language has evolved over time to fit new social constructs to understand how far we've devolved. It only took two short years to convince an entire country to refer to illegal aliens as migrants. With buy-in from corporate media, it's been easy to shift the narrative as long as we've adapted to their language. It's imperative that we recognize how subtle changes in language lead to changes in perception. This is how you pervert a nation over time. The shift will become so deeply ingrained in the DNA of our culture that there won't be enough people who remember a time before. As time goes on, those who remain will be like divers at the bottom of the ocean, tethered to memories of freedom but constantly surrounded by wreckage.

THE ENEMY DOESN'T
CARE ABOUT
YOUR FEELINGS

They'd brought him straight from prison. He was plain looking, midthirties, underwhelming in most respects. He was
educated, a PhD from Baghdad University, in fact. His eyes
were keen with intellect, and he didn't betray himself like I thought
he would, especially given the beatings. Iraqi prison wasn't safe for
a man who killed his own people, so he bet his life he'd be safer
with us. Funny how even our enemies know the code we live by is
stronger. Now he was desperate for a deal, and we were hungry for
justice that wasn't even ours to mete out. Months prior, I had voiced
my suspicions the two helicopters had never collided, their metal
carcasses strewn across the desert while uniforms knocked on front
doors thousands of miles away. We'd dug through the rubble, sifting

through charred debris to find twisted pieces of a heinous puzzle. If you know what to look for, a bombmaker's craftmanship can be as unique as a fingerprint. Those fragments held forensic clues that eventually led us to him after a rocket attack on a local bazaar. Now, he sat across the table looking at me with a steady gaze, trying his best to find common ground. Like we were two guys passing the time talking about our families. The same children spoken of with affection could have just as easily been walking hand in hand with their mother at the bombed bazaar. His efforts to humanize himself, however, inwardly disgusted me. I couldn't reconcile the man in front of me with someone who could care about anything outside of his own self-interests. He had no care for the women and children he'd murdered, and even less for the aircrew long draped in the stars and stripes and buried back home. He had no concern for the future of his country, the destruction he continued to facilitate keeping them in perpetual chaos. It didn't escape me his ability to divorce himself from the destruction until brutally confronted with his crimes in prison. He was happy to profit from death until the threat of death finally came knocking. But I pretended he wasn't a monster and let the conversation through the interpreter continue, unrushed. As he unapologetically shared the details of his crimes, I silently counted the minutes until I could walk out of that Ramadi police station and leave him to his consequences.

Choosing to live a dangerous life, one dedicated to sacrifice instead of self-interest, means there are no safe spaces. In war, as much as in practice, there's no room for hurt feelings or entitlement. The seas are unforgiving, and they don't give a damn how you identify. Feelings are irrelevant when an enemy is plotting your final breath while you're still waking up in the morning. People should be more curious why so many of us fight for objective truth, why we reject subjectivity over historical veracity. The simple answer is that an intimate relationship with death and evil is a cruel but instructive teacher. What we've seen resting at the bottom of the ocean or in the aftermath of an Improvised Explosive Device (IED) either breaks us or strengthens us. The former is a fierce battle, the latter a daily choice. We couldn't choose what we saw or did, but we've had to find ways to make peace with it in the years that followed while helping our brothers and sisters do the same. It stretches you to the end of who you think you are and then the only choice left is to step off the ledge or find a new path. For those of us who fought during years of conflict, being anchored was the key to enduring years of constant loss and family separation. My anchor was faith, and faith eventually taught me to revere truth. And not "my truth" in the self-serving, narcissistic way ideologues peddle sound bites to silence opposition, but commonsense truth divorced from emotional, hyperbolic rhetoric. This same, nonsensical rhetoric has slowly infiltrated our military, finally culminating in policies that arrogantly place activism before mission. In our singular most consequential federally run program, one that should and must remain apolitical in nature, an agenda having little to do with national security weakens our readiness around the globe.

I'd be remiss if I didn't again mention the DEI influence in our armed forces. I've had the privilege of mentoring young men and women both inside and outside the military for many years. As a member of the United States Naval Academy Minority Association, I've had a front row seat to the military's diversity, equity, and inclusion agenda, and it gives me tremendous pause. The hyper-focus on diversity in one of the most diverse workforces in the nation is inauthentic. And as an aside, it's important to note the federal government continues to cherry-pick preferential minority groups with no statistical basis or overall advantage to the military in general. For example, if I owned a lactation consulting business, specializing in in-home visits for new mothers, and hired a predominantly male staff for the explicit purpose of promoting diversity, that decision may not benefit the customer and my actions were only to reinforce my own ideology. However, if a poll of new mothers indicated they preferred male-assisted breastfeeding and other newborn needs, then a change may be warranted, and the male staff justified. But like the military's current fascination with gender and race, an ideological position does not equate a positive outcome. American taxpayers deserve a fighting force that is trained to carry out their specific mission based on metrics that are not defined by preferences or politics. It doesn't mean that the military shouldn't provide outreach to a variety of communities promoting the benefits of volunteer service in order to engage and recruit from diverse groups. Our priority should be to recruit men and women who have diverse life experiences and skills that will strengthen and challenge their fellow service members in the field. The men and women who had the most influence on my career were radically different in background and upbringing, each drawing from a wealth of experience and knowledge both personally and professionally to guide me in my growth as an officer.

Many friends and colleagues have asked why I continue to participate in conversations promoting the DEI agenda when it is so clearly antithetical to the military's overall mission and best practices. The answer lies in decades of hardworking, conservative Americans refraining from engaging institutions or organizations that espouse viewpoints that stand in stark contrast to the American dream. I contend we arrived at this level of insanity because most of us kept our head down while supporting our families, hoping with every election cycle someone would become the face of common sense and reason. As I transitioned from a military to civilian career, I realized how important it was that someone such as myself, with a diverse background both personally and professionally, remind our next generation of military leaders that true diversity begins in the mind. Over the past several years, the military has created an environment where men and women are taught to second-guess their instincts because we've convinced them that facts don't matter. We've resorted to a level of national gaslighting that blunts their capacity to access truth for fear of social outrage or retribution. It's a dangerous trend that will inevitably have a dramatic impact on our armed forces. I see it when I talk to future military officers who struggle to formulate the words to question the current ideology because they're intrinsically aware of the backlash. They see the toxic mischaracterization of truth but don't want to be canceled, even by their own military leadership, and it's ruining their ability to utilize fact and reason to grow into what we need them to be: strong, decisive leaders. What is rarely part of the conversation, what is so crucial but gets drowned out by the hyperfocus of race, gender, and identity, is that the battlefield of the mind is where wars start and end. And when they're young and still figuring out how to lead, questioning the decision-making process shouldn't always be discouraged because following orders is not the same as blind, naive obedience. If we berate them into submission, convincing them a biological man can become equal to a biological woman or that white people are systemically racist yet still expect them to become competent, critical thinkers capable of leading Teams or driving ships, we've devolved into delusion. Instead of expecting them to stand up for what is right, we're teaching them to stand for what is acceptable. We're not raising warriors; we're cultivating an army of hybrids who will wear the uniform but conform to the political machine. If we don't reverse this trend of putting ideology before the mission—and make no mistake the mission of the military is to win wars—we will lose at home and abroad. We will lose everything that has made America the beacon of hope for the rest of the world.

Although the interrogation in Ramadi was not my first or last, it certainly influenced my personal worldview. It hardened me in a way I didn't anticipate. I think that happens when you're face-to-face with evil, but it was a revelation I pondered for many years to come. I finished that particular deployment, in part, training judges and lawyers to utilize biometric technology and forensic evidence to prosecute accused terrorists who used IEDs to further their radical cause. What I took away from the bombmaker, in addition to his lack of conscience and accountability, was that he didn't care what I looked like. He certainly didn't care how I identified. His was a hate sewn into the fabric of his conscience. As hard as he tried to be friendly and courteous, he could not hide the contempt simmering quietly below the surface, and it had nothing to do with my slanted eyes or the color of my skin. It had everything to do with the flag on my shoulder. It's a lesson that should be taught at every boot camp, ROTC and OSC program, as well as every military academy: the enemy does not care how you feel. They hate us because we represent freedom, and by extension, they will try and kill you for it. This farce to push pronouns and actively celebrate certain lifestyles will get our people killed when it takes money and time away from operational readiness. Its focus on individuality over unit preparedness will fracture the cohesiveness necessary to overcome the challenges of war. And if our current geopolitical climate has demonstrated anything, a war is coming.

As our adversaries across the globe, particularly China, amass fleets and expand their global footprint, the United States struggles to contain the hemorrhage of first responders—vital for our safety at home while also convincing a new generation to serve. In the same way, but on a larger scale, the military is suffering a recruiting crisis so dramatic that legislators in Washington are finally demanding answers. My question is this: Does Washington really want answers when they have been a part of the problem? From my perspective, the lack of willing enlistees is threefold: we have abandoned our principles as a nation, demonized the alpha-warriors necessary to lead, and abandoned the same men and women who swore to protect and defend a country they love more than their own lives. This opinion may not be popular—fortunately I stopped caring a long time ago—but it's a truth understood by many of our fellow Soldiers, Sailors, Airmen, Marines, and Coastguardsmen. I'll add to that a country in conflict for over twenty years without a balanced budget, operating within rules of engagement created by bureaucrats in Washington who wouldn't dare lift a pen to support the middle class let alone a rifle. The only way to find a solution is through hard truths that cannot be glossed over to salvage stars or position.

As long as the military pursues a social justice agenda, even going so far as promoting the "white rage" narrative, recruiting numbers will continue to plummet. When the Department of Defense (DOD) makes no effort to distinguish racist neo-Nazis from "right-wing extremists," the interchangeable vernacular becomes problematic in rooting out real instances of hate and violence while equally suggesting a problem with conservative, white men. It's a juxtaposition that points a finger at one demographic regardless of context or continuity. When I ran for Congress, I was aggressively labeled a "right-wing extremist." A commercial said so, so it must be true. But in all seriousness, these were the same people who thanked me for my service only months before yet worked night and day to assassinate my character once my ideals didn't fall in line with theirs. The term has been used to add fuel to a political fire, and the military gave it official legs. Gone are the days when being proud to be an American is a positive—in fact, now it's considered taboo, radical even. Who wants to volunteer for a military that doesn't take every opportunity to highlight its own strength? And not the jets and missiles. The strength of the military is in her people. People who sacrifice and toil at a job that pays zero overtime and has lifelong physical and mental health consequences. Those who have served did so because we loved the men and women who served beside us and wearing the cloth of our nation meant serving a purpose higher than ourselves. Black, white, yellow, brown, our common bond is our love of country and the small privilege to guarantee freedom for the next generation. In a stunning reversal, the principles of life, liberty, and the pursuit of happiness are now considered fringe. The constant pressure on our young people to conform to anti-American sentiment is a continued, unspoken impediment to recruitment. Extremist? That's not a message that sells. The whole world knows it, and the numbers prove it.

It takes a certain kind of person to raise their right hand and swear an oath to defend and protect the Constitution from all enemies foreign and domestic. Especially when you consider the punishing training required for special programs throughout each branch of the military. Specialized units naturally attract alpha males and females and weed out glory seekers and medal hunters. They are likely to push themselves beyond what most would consider normal and are, most importantly, willing to learn humility in the process. When I graduated from Explosive Ordnance Disposal (EOD) school, it was two days after the 9/11 attacks. In a matter of hours, the trajectory of our lives and careers changed forever. We couldn't have known what we would endure or who we would lose. We couldn't have known that years of deployments would tear apart marriages and destroy families. Who could have anticipated the twenty-two veterans a day who now die by suicide? But the training had prepared us, and I believe we were the right people at the right time to serve a hurting nation. Now, we scoff at the alpha male and label masculinity toxic when wars have been won by the very spirit of men willing to "do violence on our behalf." The last thing this country needs are weak-kneed men and women whose willingness to serve is predicated on a desire to transform the military from an exclusive to an inclusive fighting force. At its core, the armed forces are exclusionary. But exclusivity by its nature sets a standard, and the standard falls directly in line with the needs of the mission at home and abroad. Those wishing to serve must meet the physical, intellectual, and mental standards because, as many of us know firsthand, deviation can impede a mission and manpower at the worst possible time. This all culminates with decisive leadership who recognizes the strength and character of people suited for service. The DOD must come to terms that intrinsically, strong men and women do not want and will not follow weak leadership. They will not sign up to follow leaders who are more comfortable in an office than they are with their men in the field. Fundamentally, our recruitment crisis is a leadership crisis. What we've witnessed over the past several years is weakness too many are simply unwilling to risk their lives for.

COVID was a turning point for thousands of active duty service members. They could not abide an organization that forced them to take part in an experimental vaccine and then went out of their way to villainize them for standing their ground. Regardless of the merits of the vaccine, each person must decide for themselves based on the information readily available if that was the right choice for them. What many didn't want was to become cannon fodder, a playground for experimentation when their personal sacrifice had already pushed them to the brink. And many will and have said, "So what, it's only a shot," or "It's the military; you have no right to a choice," and it's certainly their right to think that. Just as it was the right of service members to question a federal mandate for an experimental medical procedure that carried no exemption. It was a slap in the face for those who fought for the right for free speech and religious freedom. There is no way to measure the damage done by the overwhelming message to take the vaccine or leave the only life you've ever known, walking away downgraded in rate or rank without retirement. It happened. A lot. I think the average

American, regardless of their opinion on the mandates, would be sickened by the extent the military went to demonize and punish service members who simply voiced their concerns. Many were threatened with dishonorable discharge by leaders who had known them for years, placing their future livelihood and family security in peril. Active duty service members who served with units through deployments were summarily shunned by leadership; the direction to the entire command was that they were persons no longer trustworthy. It has tarnished the reputation of the military on a scale no one could have anticipated and deterred those who treasure freedom from ever signing on the dotted line. COVID restrictions put an end to generational military service. Already a precious commodity, recruitment numbers tell the tale of families who proudly served over the course of decades discouraging their children and grandchildren from doing the same. They feel cheated and wronged by military leadership and have advised their own families to find a profession that respects choice and personal autonomy.

Regardless of personal opinion, the fact is that senior military leadership critically mishandled the COVID-19 pandemic, with a young, statistically healthy military. When natural immunity and the contribution of comorbidities weren't even factored into mandate policy, the federal government failed to convince service members that the mission came before Washington bureaucracy—especially when elected officials flaunted breaking the rules themselves but still kept their jobs and retirement. Many who willingly took the vaccine now question whether political expediency, and not health or military readiness, was the priority of military brass. It seems no one in the Pentagon considered the consequences of asking a young, healthy fighting force to mask and vaccinate even when the emerging science did not support a grave necessity. This was a lesson in understanding perception equals reality. If the same people who are most likely to raise their hand and swear to protect and defend the Constitution were the same people questioning the motivations of blanket lockdowns, vaccine mandates, and unflinchingly rigid masking, what did we think would happen? Every branch of the military makes compelling, patriotic commercials that dare young Americans to live a life of fearless adventure in the United States military. And then COVID came. Gone is the fierce, independent spirit needed to be a part of the world's strongest fighting force. Instead, overnight, the military projected a message of fear, and it was demonstrated in the way they assassinated the character of our own people. The message was suddenly, put on a mask, take your shot, and shut the hell up or we will ruin you. Don't dare file a religious exemption because it won't even make it up the chain of command. You can decide to die for your country, but you can't decide what to put in your body. Until leadership starts asking the right questions and recognizes the damage done during the pandemic, I don't know how we meet recruitment needs for the foreseeable future.

Finally, we come to August 2021. I've already shared my thoughts about the growing sentiment of distrust and why rigid pandemic policies hurt recruitment. The fall of Afghanistan was not only the nail in our recruitment coffin, but it also solidified the uneasiness that politics was being prioritized over lives. When our nation asks young men and women to serve, there's an unspoken understanding that their leadership will have their back. That we send men and women in harm's way with every tool necessary to return home to their families with the mission successfully completed. If they work hard, dedicate themselves to the task before them, and take advantage of every opportunity available, their success can have an upward trajectory setting them on a path of success for a lifetime. When the leadership is good, and I can't stress enough that so often it is, this is the natural order of things. One of the most fulfilling jobs I had in the Navy was as a Commanding

Officer. I was acutely aware every day of both the privilege and consequence of being in a trusted position. The burden and responsibility of command is a sacred trust which made, in my estimation, the failure in Afghanistan even more egregious.

Before I left Afghanistan six months prior to the fall it was, overall, stable. I traveled extensively throughout the country as the Director of Counter Improvised Threat and Advisor to Afghan National Defense Security Forces. I had been to Kabul, conducting a no-notice, large-scale IED detonation drill at Abbey Gate, based on intelligence sourced from my special forces advisors. Because of that intel, it was imperative we tested the capacity of a multilingual, multinational force's ability to respond to an IED threat or detonation. Who could have imagined only months later, eleven Marines, one Sailor, and one Soldier would die at that gate. It's horrific to still think about and the months following that devastating day I questioned whether I'd done enough to prepare those on the ground. I came home in January, confident that while we would still reserve a small footprint, I would not see the mountains or inhale the dust of Afghanistan again. It had been twenty years, trillions of dollars, and thousands of lives lost. Watching the surrender of Afghanistan to the Taliban play out on television was an experience I will not soon forget. The Afghan government dissolved; panic ensued with families surging Hamid Karzai International Airport to escape the Taliban's imminent arrival. We watched as mothers thrust wailing babies at Marines and young men plummeted to their death from the landing gear of a C-17 after takeoff. It reminded me of footage of the fall of Saigon, tragic in every sense of the word.

But what we didn't see was even worse. Most of America doesn't know the Taliban lined up men and women against the airport wall and executed them while our military was told to stand down. The news didn't show our government give the Taliban lists of the names of men and women who spent twenty years risking their lives assisting our military over twenty years. They were promised the hope of a new life, and what they received in return was worse than abandonment. It was betrayal. After the withdrawal, when Americans were left behind, trapped and forced into hiding, the Biden Administration never uttered one word about the violence perpetrated on women who had taken leadership roles both in government and law enforcement. They didn't bat an eye at the little girls banned from schools and forced into marriage with old men. The daily reports we received were bleak. There were victories, but they had nothing to do with the efforts of the State Department. It was private partnerships led by American patriots, mostly former military, who understood the gravity of the reckless withdrawal. This failure of leadership cost our nation thirteen young lives, our national reputation, and the reversal of twenty years of human rights in a country where women had been oppressed and marginalized for centuries. We left behind allies, interpreters, and American citizens all due to a feckless Commander in Chief. When the bodies arrived at Dover, my wife and I watched in silence from our family room. Our hands gripped, unable to hold back tears as they loaded casket after casket into black vans. And there stood the President of the United States, checking his watch over and over and over again while devastated families grieved for a loss many know was preventable. There are very few times in my life when I have been so genuinely disgusted.

Every young person in the nation watched our government abandon Americans to an unknown fate with a regime who had worked tirelessly to kill our people for decades. Our State Department made excuses and played semantics as they explained away their reasons for leaving behind thousands of Special Interest Visa holders. We'd promised them a better life for their sacrifice and service to our country when we needed their expertise and guidance most. To those of us who served with them, the fallout was unacceptable, and we did our best in the months and year after to right many of those wrongs. But our work after the fall of Kabul will not erase the images of death and terror that continue to play out in Afghanistan. A strong military requires leadership that will not abandon their principles for political expediency. Our future service members should feel confident that the orders they're given are orders their leadership would be willing to take and execute on the ground themselves. The burden of leadership is heavy, and the cost is displayed row after row in Arlington National Cemetery. Those who have had the privilege know its weight intimately because it serves as a reminder that our position is never given but earned, as is the trust of those we command.

Everything is a lesson. We either take our experiences, our failures and flaws, and apply them to life or we allow them to consume us. The military was where I learned to be a man worthy of being a husband and father and, in many ways, a better son to parents who sacrificed so I could thrive in freedom. It taught me sacrifice and self-control. The constant change, the sheer unpredictability associated with most facets of military life, forced me to consider the bigger picture outside of my own wants and needs. It wasn't always a picture I agreed with, but the tenacity to excel for the sake of people under my command, along with the mission, became prioritized over bureaucratic red tape. Prioritizing personal and professional growth over my circumstances kept me from indulging the temptation to chase rank and title at the expense of my family. Maturity and mentorship helped me see that along the way, my success was not my own. I owed much of who I became as a military officer to men and women who expected excellence and challenged me to be better. What we're witnessing now is very senior military leadership without the same inclinations. Facing disastrous recruiting numbers, one would assume there would be an awakening, if not by choice, then by necessity. Coupled with an aging fleet, budget limitations, and adversaries who have utilized technology and access to steal our intellectual property to boost their military might, the fate of our national security is tenuous.

Our men and women in uniform are some of the finest human beings I have ever known. They are tenacious, resilient, and deeply devoted to the number one priority of our federal government: to ensure the safety and security of this nation. Although the current outlook on recruiting looks bleak, there are reasons for hope. While many bemoan the current generation, I believe there is greatness on the horizon because they are the descendants of brave and heroic warfighters. The same fighting spirit that raised all but two ships from Pearl Harbor, refitted them for war, and sent them back out to sea to fight the same enemy who tried to destroy them lives in our young men and women today. The men who fought in the jungles of Vietnam risking everything for the friend on their left and right now have grandchildren who will hear their stories. We have an obligation to encourage them, to reignite a fire we hope has not been fully extinguished at the hands of a consuming social justice agenda. It is incumbent on all of us to tell our stories in our communities, demonstrating our love of country through our actions to inspire those who will one day, for better or worse, become leaders in our armed forces.

The time for staying silent is over. This generation deserves our wisdom, guidance, and passion. If you have served or are currently serving, offer to speak of your experiences to Boy Scout Troops, after-school clubs, or homeschool groups. Become active in your local government or veteran's groups. Invest your time in the JROTC program or mentor teens who are in a single-parent home. Leadership will eventually change, as it always does, and we can help change the trajectory of our nation one person at a time. It really can be that simple. For me, it was Marines on a wall when I was eight. For someone else it may be the grandpa who speaks at a high school assembly about their experiences as a fighter pilot or an aunt who deployed on a nuclear submarine. We must offer a replacement for the incessant garbage they hear from social media because they are smart and they are paying attention. The American spirit is the enemy of injustice and the greatest deterrent of war. I see it in young men and women like my son who have chosen to serve knowing the alternative is to allow evil to reign unopposed in the world. Peace through strength at all costs but if that fails, an Army, Navy, Air Force, and Marine Corps unwavering in their resolve for victory. Success is not from never failing; it is from rising after every fall.

ON GOD AND POLITICS

"Aren't you afraid to die, XO?" Launched by insurgents, rockets and mortars pounded the perimeter of the base. As the alarm blared, echoing throughout the hundred-acre forward operating base, the speaker calmly announced, "Incoming, incoming, incoming." Body armor already heavy on my shoulders, pistol strapped to my leg and rifle in my hand, my feet kicked up dust as I strode toward the Command Post. Ordering our armored gunboats to intercept the insurgents before they retreated across the border to Iran, I grabbed my Chief Petty Officer and the first ATV we could find to begin our accountability search. Even though hell was raining down on us, I was relieved to be in the open air and out of the stifling Conex box I slept in for a few meager hours a day. It felt like a makeshift coffin, and I didn't want to relive the experience of getting blown out of my bed again. As we drove, my eyes constantly scanning, I contemplated his question. This unit was different than the Teams I'd led and worked with over the past several years. For many of them, the experience was unsettling in ways I could not have prepared them for. The incessant rocket attacks, IEDs, and heightened current of nervous energy during operations outside the wire, jarred their sense of reality and safety. As operators, most of us learned to work through those feelings in our own time, some managing them better than others. I'd already been in the sand box and relied on my ability to siphon any trepidation through a filter of faith while honing muscle memory and instinct. I also learned to compartmentalize, ignoring the peripheral destruction around me so I could quickly identify the solution in front of me.

Being a bomb tech isn't about having steady hands; it's about being disciplined enough to have a steady mind. The men I led that deployment wanted to know my secret for remaining calm when everything seemed like it could go very wrong. The answer to his question, although sincere, was not original. Stonewall Jackson perfectly encapsulated my feelings about death and dying on the battlefield, and it was his sentiment I chose to paraphrase. My God is so powerful, I told him, that I was just as safe there as I was in my own bed at home. Only Christ knew my end just as only He had known my beginning. I was a man who had been born and raised on foreign soil only to end up living in the freest country on earth. To me, it was, and continues to be, a miracle only God could have orchestrated. Surely I could trust Him with my life even when facing the most evil of men. What mattered most was not the timing of my death, over which I had no control, but where I would spend eternity. I was a man who knew where I was going and trusted God with the end as much as the present. My only regret would be leaving my wife to raise our children alone. It was hard to think about them not knowing or remembering me, but even in that, I had no doubt God would provide for them in my absence. The thoughts we shared weaving throughout the base lasted beyond that ATV ride. Everyone safe and accounted for, conversations about God continued until we went our separate ways almost eighteen months later. Faith, in its simplest form, isn't just a belief. It's a roadmap. Mine was paved through circumstances that could have broken my spirit or instilled in me a sense of bitterness and shame. But God had better plans.

As a kid, when my classmates found out I was in martial arts, I was often challenged to fight. Sometimes for fun, sometimes not. But the challengers, regardless of intention, boldly asserted the same rule: I couldn't use martial arts against them or to defend myself. To me, it was a ridiculous request. I wouldn't turn off that part of me. They were asking me to restrain myself for their gain and my disadvantage; my response to them was simple. I wasn't afraid to fight, but I certainly wouldn't choose to weaken myself to satisfy them. Surprised by my refusal, they eventually stopped asking even though I was almost always smaller in stature. It wasn't until the Academy that I was given a chance to fight outside a strict, competitive environment. Every Midshipman, both male and female, is required to take a boxing course. Because of my experience as a kickboxer, I approached the boxing coach and asked if he would allow me to validate the class. This request to test out of a course was commonplace in both academics and sports. Midshipmen who had extracurricular experience or prior advance placement could request testing or validation in order to fulfill the class requirement. The coach simply laughed. Kickboxing wasn't even close to boxing, he said. He ordered me to the ring, obviously wanting to prove a point when he paired me with a much bigger upperclassman who had been on the team for two years. Maybe he hoped I would learn a swift lesson in humility and leave with my tail tucked between my legs. I was warned only to use my fists and keep my feet on the floor. To me it was just one more fight, and I spared no time sizing up the upperclassman. As soon as the bell rang, I launched myself at him. After forty-five seconds, my opponent dropped his arms, and I reacted with calculated speed. I executed two punches and a spinning backfist to the head in quick succession, dropping him to the ground. The coach shouted in protest, angrily ordered me out of the ring, and I spent the rest of the term in his class. But the funny thing was, by the end of the year, the coach had asked several times if I would join the team. My instinct gave me an edge, even if I wasn't his kind of boxer. I politely declined, but it taught me a valuable lesson: don't pretend to be someone you're not. Be content with who you are, not who everyone wants you to be, and don't separate the most important parts of yourself to appease people.

If you're anything like me, you can no more separate your faith from everyday life than you could fight without using past experience or training. We weren't born with layers to be peeled and tucked away for public convenience. I am not a man who changes what I believe or how I speak based on my audience. Faith is not an outer shell we can discard once we exit our churches, synagogues, mosques, and temples. Too many of us act this way, and maybe that's why the expectation has prevailed. Millions of us have been transformed by faith, so much so that our worldview is shaped and guided by tenets that become guiding principles for life. And while politicians in Washington have tried desperately to convince us that God must be wholly separated from government in order to preserve liberty, the truth is that a society void of faith is destined to fail. Ignoring the reality that our laws are an extension of Judeo-Christian values is disingenuous and dangerous. Activists and elitists, by design, have systematically warped society's perception of faith and morality, in turn diminishing its relevance in a productive, civilized society. Currently, the activist agenda uses emotional blackmail on the back of historical shame as a sucker punch for anyone who disagrees with the activists' propaganda. Their new faith of fluid morality is steeped in subjective tolerance utterly beholden to the whims of a select minority. What is good is now evil, and what is evil is repackaged as good. Underwear-clad men wearing prosthetic genitalia while gyrating sexually in front of small children should always be offensive and intolerable regardless of the occasion or location. Now we're supposed to pretend this same exact action is abhorrent and indecent at a public playground but acceptable at a parade or on a stage. Not only is it illogical, but it is purposefully deceitful. This is more than a slippery slope. It's mental gymnastics on a radical level that desensitizes common decency with the ultimate goal of compartmentalizing morality. This is what passivism encouraged, and this is what we must endeavor to undo. Those of us who subscribe to faith and objective truth know that this display can't be both good and bad at the same time. Take theft as another example. Theft through government waste and outrageous spending, even when passed through legislation, is as immoral as a person who steals from a store at knifepoint. Just because we now tolerate one and not the other doesn't negate the fact that the act itself should be morally repugnant and leads to economic decline. Many years ago, a certain group of fiery men fought a war against illegal taxation and representation, yet somehow we've become immune and even accepting of our bloated, wasteful government. Times change, but the principles that were the foundation of the most innovative and free country in the world should not. It's a long time coming for God's people to stop turning a blind eye to the degradation of truth and morality. If we don't, we will have generations of Americans separated far enough from truth that the very notion will be rejected as antiquated and frivolous. An exceptionally poor outcome for a nation that is the benefactor of tremendous courage but unwilling to demonstrate the same in order to keep it.

One of the greatest lies perpetuated in American history is that faith and religion have no place in public. Not in our schools, not in culture, and certainly not in the way we govern. In our efforts to reach the culture, sadly, we became the culture and are now fighting a battle we may not have the stomach to win. As Christians, specifically, we allowed ourselves to be shamed into submission. For years we listened to pop psychologists tell us to keep the peace at all costs. In particular, families became the target for the tolerance propaganda machine. Never discuss religion or politics because the dinner table was no place for challenging discourse or disagreement. Healthy debate and verbal sparring over passed dishes quickly became a mortal sin and with it the time-honored tradition of agreeing to disagree. In fact, the effort to remove faith and politics from the family table worked so well that we've forgotten what it feels like to be wrong among the people who know and love us best. Gone is the practice of being quick to listen and slow to speak. Ushered in is the elevated, hyperemotional state of being offended when the truth doesn't conform to a personal narrative. Facts matter far less than feelings these days. Daytime talk show therapists and, incredibly, even pastors in the pulpit politely suggested we restrain ourselves from speaking about issues that created discomfort for the listener. It was packaged as loving, but the practice of selective silence has had a remarkably dark effect on our society. What we were really being told was to leave our faith at the door without realizing it would never end there. As conservatives and Christians, we packed up our principles and collectively committed to private faith while the culture rushed forward without a whisper of input. It was so easy to be quiet that it didn't even feel wrong. Don't push back and God will take care of the rest. That's true. He will and He does. Especially when His people ignore the injustice in front of them but feast at the table laid before them. Make no mistake, blissful ignorance is no longer a good-enough excuse to remain silent. But this is the genesis of the apathy and divisiveness we're experiencing in our country.

We've been told on all fronts that moral issues are in fact political, and now any subject deemed political is inappropriate in most spaces. Your opinions and facts are no longer welcome. You know that sharing concerns over growing violence in the United States and how best to defend your family is not welcome at Thanksgiving dinner. You don't believe school libraries should be a safe haven for pornographic reading material under the guise of inclusion but don't want to be called a bigot over dessert. How many people have a family member who is no longer speaking to them because of a difference of opinion over a shot in the arm? At some point, we have all witnessed someone twist themselves around a conversation in order to refrain from the mere appearance of offence. And it isn't solely a Democrat or Republican issue; it's a natural by-product of political ideology replacing that still small voice. When we're externally motivated by subjective talking points instead of facts, not only do we rob ourselves of the opportunity to model integrity, we replace moral authority with position, power, and influence. During the most recent confirmation hearing to the Supreme Court, I watched as Judge Ketanji Brown Jackson demonstrated remarkable verbal jiu-jitsu in order to avoid defining womanhood. It was a sight to behold, startling really, and I don't believe anyone who watched her testimony believed she didn't know the factual answer to that question. In front of country, she was willing to deny her own intelligence, to the point of perjury, to fit a narrative that conflicts not only with common sense but also science. The problem with her answer was that it revealed a level of willful deception while exposing her personal motivation. We can speak to the merits of different interpretations of the law all day, but we must agree that every decision is predicated on truth. Can cases brought before the Supreme Court be adjudicated fairly when one Justice has publicly proclaimed that she, as a woman, can't define a woman? What if the case determines matters of discrimination against a particular sex and has ramifications for future generations? We've all seen cases we know will affect our children, and it's disheartening to see political maneuvering seep into the robes of our highest court in the land. This is why we cannot continue to perpetuate the continued lie that moral issues are intrinsically linked to politics and therefore unsuitable for consumption in public spaces. Though hailed as political, these are meaningful issues of morality serving as the continued building blocks of our nation.

When the church deemed abortion a political issue instead of a human rights issue, the bright flame of the church began to flicker. When church leaders dare not advocate for women and children on Sunday, it gives people of faith permission to uncouple their conscience from the reality of the Gospel the rest of the week. We convinced ourselves that we didn't have to stand for the unborn in public, as long as God knew how we really felt in private. But we haven't been called to live life quietly in the back row. In fact, we are called by God, through faith, to share and serve even to the point of discomfort. If we can't do that, how can we possibly stand against the utter insanity we're witnessing in our country today? If God's commandments are not the litmus test for morality, then morality will not stand against the rising influence of modern secular humanism in an increasingly divided country. Objective truth will no longer anchor the guiding principles of our nation because it will have been allowed to evolve. Loving our neighbor as ourselves does not mean subjugating society to immorality just so we can say we stayed above the fray. Christians in particular failed to understand that love can't always be separated from offense. Even spoken with compassion, the truth can be offensive, but it doesn't make it wrong. Liberal theology continues to proselytize the idealistic notion of separating faith from political discourse, refraining from the ugliness, and praying that God moves so we don't have to. It's a contrary position, and I object to the nonsensical idea that

Christians must abstain from the political arena because it's a nasty business. Nowhere in His word does God command us to compartmentalize life based on cultural trends. Morality is already deeply woven into our founding documents and law. Our engagement should be significant enough that it compels societal self-reflection and authentic growth toward a more perfect union. Instead of removing ourselves, we should have been willing to be an example even if it meant suffering under the piercing weight of slings and arrows. But because we took that intentional step backward, those of us committed to moving forward in faith and politics now do so under a system expertly poised and willing to oppress, demonize, and prosecute with incredible effectiveness. There is a reason why those who control the narrative have the most influence. They use it to take up enough space that it leaves no room for discourse or dissent. Eventually, whatever the issue is, whether or not we agree with it, actually becomes a part of everyday life. Imagine what the narrative would be if Christians had come together as a cohesive community and advocated for life publicly over the past thirty or forty years. Yes, there were amazing examples of men and women serving their communities to advocate for the life of women and children, but they were the exception not the rule. The silence of the church created a vacuum that allowed politicians to corrupt and pervert the truth.

There's a temptation to define ourselves politically in an attempt to justify ourselves morally. This viscous cycle only continues to assert the belief that morality is purely political instead of recognizing the objective nature of right and wrong on which the basis of morality hinges. But we get so wrapped up in left or right that we forget we're really talking about people. We forget that moral authority—not superiority—continues to be the catalyst of free societies where the individual is valued over the collective. Unencumbered by mob rule, individual liberty began with the belief that all men were created equal. Not because the government granted it, but because our Founders acknowledged that there could be no higher authority than God. Our Constitutional Republic, established in fundamental human rights, was not a system of governance created for perfect people, but instead with perfect understanding of the flawed nature of man. Therefore, it's reasonable to assume that our Founders were not only aware of, but provided a path for, the extinction of America's most egregious sins. All of which were eventually outlawed because they were antithetical to the basic tenet that we are endowed by our Creator to live freely. It acknowledged we were created equally not because of who we are but because of who God is. Faith-informed reasoning has always been a relevant part of the legislative process, and we see the fruit of it daily.

When I ran for office, it was clear to me that the talking points on both sides were only designed to hurt the opponent and win elections. While Americans are left to sift through the rubble of ridiculous name-calling, real issues with real consequences are patently ignored. My opponent knew I wasn't an anti-woman, far-right, violent extremist. She knew I was a father, husband, and decorated combat veteran deeply devoted to my faith. But she also knew that, statistically, Americans are more likely to react when their wallet is tied to their emotions. We say we can't stand politicians who use dirty tactics, but the numbers don't lie. We may say it with our mouths, but our wallets tell a completely different story. Outrage sells, and we are its number one consumer. It's why we remained committed to abstaining from personal attacks on the campaign trail. I would be lying if I didn't say I was tempted. It's not easy to be attacked or to have your family attacked just because you desire public service on the opposite side of the aisle. As a person who was in service my whole life, in many ways this seemed like a natural next step when I realized we were losing our country to the growing trend of socialism. It wasn't to best Democrats; it was to become a reasonable voice in a sea of political hysteria. I'm a doer. When I see a need I jump in and commit myself, especially now when our country is at a tipping point. Unfortunately, politics is not the place for logic and reason, but it should be. We need men and women who are willing to stand before their constituents and have the integrity to debate the facts without outlandish rhetoric. If we want a return to civility, it must begin with us, and that is what I did. Day in and day out I observed my opponent override her own sense of decency, just as many politicians do, in order to win. It certainly gave me perspective, and the contrast between our two campaigns was not lost on the electorate. Eight months later, I still have people stop me and thank me for running a positive campaign that avoided the negative back-and-forth they so often see. Even Democrats tell me that while they didn't vote for me, they recognized I ran an honorable race. I didn't have their vote, but I had their respect. Maybe to some this doesn't matter if the result is loss. I think too many are willing to undermine their own values if the outcome is a win. Politics is all about the ends justifying the means. But to me, it meant that I could hold my head high in my community and continue to serve in my own way. That regardless of politics, my neighbors, coworkers, and even strangers would still trust me to be fair and compassionate. They still trusted me to be invited into their circumstances, and that is a blessing itself. This is why a foundation of faith matters.

This chapter, by far, has been the most difficult to write. We are living in a time when most people have been convinced that having faith also means the inability to objectively respect the rule of law. It's a mischaracterization that festers and continues to fuel division. This is why politicians continue to label every person on the opposite side of the political spectrum with the same repetitive, heinous names. It doesn't matter that I am a refugee and minority; they will still say I am a racist and bigot because of what I believe even though my belief system has not changed. While I was in uniform, I was someone to be applauded for my bravery and courage (ridiculous, I was only doing my job); three months later, however, I was suddenly a threat to democracy. This is why it's important to remain steadfast in our beliefs—especially when it comes to faith. I was okay with being the wrong kind of boxer just like I'm okay with aspiring to public service as a Christian. It's harder than it sounds, I know. As a part of the first generation that shunned any talk of faith and politics, it suited me fine most of my military career. Although I had my personal convictions and leaned conservative, I was not what you would consider a political person. But that changed when I finally saw a stark and precarious future for our kids. It changed me because what I was being told was political was an obvious breakdown in morality across every spectrum of society. It had nothing to do with politics and everything to do with redefining decency and common sense. And maybe I was too busy fighting for our country, but when did we decide it's better to burn everything to the ground than come to the table and debate? When did we decide our country wasn't worth the painstaking art of compromise? Real life encourages a real exchange of ideas, yet it's discouraged. During deployments, we often spoke of faith and politics, and there was no anger or hostility. My Sailors wanted to know my thoughts and how I framed my belief system, and I was honest. It was a privilege to share with them and have them share their experiences with me. It increased my understanding of the human condition in a way that made me a better man over time.

When I say the military is the most diverse job creator in America, I mean it. I had the pleasure of serving with men and women who survived circumstances I could barely fathom, and it was humbling to walk with them through some of the hardest parts of life. Their strength and commitment to faith during incredible adversity were an encouragement and inspiration, and it opened my eyes to the ways truth always makes a way for the light. My job was to lead to the best of my ability while understanding and respecting the boundaries of my authority. My faith required it, and I believe everyone was better for it. As a leader, I had Sailors who requested leave to participate in their Wiccan holiday and those who requested accommodations to pray at a certain time during the day. There were Sailors who fasted during rigorous, energy-depleting training and those who believed the dirt in the ground was finality personified. I served with liberals, independents, conservatives, and those who were outspoken and opinionated about a host of other issues unrelated to politics. It's so unlike my experiences in the civilian world now, that there are times I miss the comradery. It was easier to be different when shared experiences equated a common perspective. That perspective wasn't being in complete agreement with one another but respecting the right to have a difference of opinion. What we could agree on, however, were issues of morality because we had seen the worst and saw clearly the difference. While compromise is important and necessary, we should also be in agreement that there are things worthy of a fight. The soul of our country depends on it.

Faith itself is the best tool for self-governance. When we think about the tens of thousands of local, state, and federal laws, it's as if nothing we do is without legal restriction. Our county just passed a ridiculous plastic bag tax, and every time I go to the grocery store, I roll my eyes at the self-checkout counter. I know I could skip the screen where I'm asked to enter the number of bags used and avoid the five-cents-per-bag tax. Who would know? But honestly, my faith prevents me from doing so. It may seem like a silly example, but it illustrates how I am restrained in the same way as the vast majority of Americans. When you have a strict, moral belief system, whatever it is, you automatically become self-governed. This is why faith and religion are so crucial to civility, common decency, and

the rule of law. Even if you are not a person who believes in organized religion, I guarantee you've developed a personal moral code
that defines your life. I hate to be the bearer of bad news, but most
of those morals are derived from the Bible; nonetheless, you believe
them to be right and for good reason. Thou shalt not murder, covet,
steal, bear false witness, and commit adultery are universal truths.
They are the foundation of our Western culture, and it is good that
people practice them for the sake of others. We should encourage
faith, not diminish its value in a free society. For example, those who
attempt to erase faith from the public square are choosing to ignore
that faith specifically was the catalyst to end slavery. Those who
fought and died for the equal rights of all men did so before there
was a law to compel them. Their endurance paved the way for legal
change and the eventual abolishment of slavery, segregation, and
tyranny. They were convicted because the obvious wrong revealed
the necessary right. Faith steeled the spines of men even on pain of
ridicule, excommunication, or death as they stood for those who
could not stand for themselves. True faith places sacrifice above self
and is vital to mankind. Think about it. If the arguments opposing
drag shows for kids, pornography, and the real biology of women
continues to dominate daily conversations without resolution, the
likelihood of regaining the narrative is slim. Right now, any moral
argument against these actions is viciously labeled hateful religious
intolerance. The case is literally being made that if you oppose the
above, regardless of whether you are Jewish, Christian, or Muslim,
then you are a bigot. Protecting children is now deemed phobic and
hateful. Your morality, which has been the norm of society for hundreds of years, is now obscene. I have seen all over the world what
it looks like to cherish children and what it looks like to exploit and
endanger them. What we're doing as a country will have generational consequences, and yet there is still more silence than outrage.
Can you imagine how far these radical agendas would have gotten

if people of faith would have rallied to school board meetings several years ago? This has been happening for quite a while. Now the question is, do you follow what is socially virtuous or morally right according to God and your conscience? Will you capitulate to political party or vote with your morality? I know I'm going to fight, and I'd like to know that I'm not doing it alone. We can't leave it up to a few people to hopefully do the right thing. We must stop asking our leaders in Washington to be elected saviors. We are a government for the people and by the people. The emphasis is on us, not them. It's our turn to dominate the narrative with truth.

I want to end with some personal encouragement. The saying goes that there is no atheist in a foxhole. That our nature is hardwired to seek and petition a Creator. I've seen it firsthand, and, like a child who cries out for his mother, so too do men instinctively seek God during seasons of deep hurt. Even the staunchest atheist, someone who rejects the overwhelming evidence for God, will cry out to Him in panic, pain, or even before death. The world's most notable atheists expressed their disbelief in God but still held out hope that He does, in fact, exist. Faith changed my life. I was raised Buddhist but never felt peace with the conditionality of that faith, and it was in a hard time that I was presented with the Gospel of Jesus. It was transformative, miraculous, and humbling. When I understood the gift of His sacrifice on the cross, I was overwhelmed, and my life has never been the same. Every single one of us was beautifully and wonderfully made. Your life is not an accident, and there is a God who longs to know you. Seek Him. I can't promise life will be easier, but I can promise that His mercies are good and the peace that surpasses all understanding will accompany you all the days of your life.

ENTITLEMENT

I held my composure until I shook the last hand, and the final diver rejoined his class. After saying goodbye to students and their families, I found my Command Master Chief (CMC), pointed to a particular graduate, and asked that he report to my office immediately. As the class celebrated and mingled, laughing with relief as they relived moments they thought would break them, I sat at my desk and took a deep breath. I replayed the moment the student, smirking, swiped the certificate from my hand before I could present it, laughed, and sauntered offstage. The audacity astounded me, and although I shouldn't have been surprised, it still caught me off-guard. Before I could decide on a course of action, the CMC and graduate arrived at my office. I directed the young man, now standing at attention in front of me, to remove the new dive pin from his chest and place it on my desk. I stood silently as tears formed and spilled down his cheeks, the silver pin making a soft clink against the wood. I could see him slowly come to the realization of what was being taken, and in that moment, I felt for him. I remembered being eighteen and filled with the overconfidence of youth. But it also wasn't lost on me that the burden of command meant identifying cracks in the foundation before they could affect the safety of an entire structure. Protocol and decorum may seem frivolous to some, but I knew from experience what a lack of humility can do to the morale of an entire unit. A sense of entitlement has no place on a team and could threaten a mission before it begins. Lives depend on the assurance that a team is cohesive, everyone watching out for the brother and sister beside them, not relying on their own bravado or high ideals. He hadn't just disrespected the school; he had disrespected his classmates and the instructors who worked tirelessly on their behalf. My job wasn't to break his spirit but to encourage a sense of honor and reverence for the work ahead of him. I made it clear that my expectation for him on their final day was no different than what was expected on the first. I picked up the pin and held it in front of him. This pin, I told him, would have to be earned every day for the rest of his career. The hard work wasn't over; in fact, it had just begun. Now, he had the difficult task of earning the respect and trust of the Soldiers who would serve alongside him. We were not entitled to respect just because we wore a dive pin, Crab, or Trident. We have a duty and an obligation to live up to the excellence the pin represents because our country deserves the very best of our talents and skills. For a second time, I placed the pin on his chest. I shook his hand and held it, looking him in the eyes and finally seeing the humility I hoped would carry him forward in success. I wished him well and told him to go and do good things for the community.

Rank, position, power. Most earn it, but along the way too many lose it. When I was a kid, awkward and trying to figure out my place in the world, I had a sense of constantly having to prove myself. Even in my small military community, there were times I couldn't escape the glaring reality that I was a minority. And not the way you might think. I didn't consider my skin color when I was in a room filled with my peers. But my unique life experiences and upbringing often made me feel set apart. How I'd grown up and the big world I'd been exposed to shaped the way I interreacted with the people around me. Even how I heard language seemed different. I didn't feel confined by the same military culture as my peers. I saw every opportunity to lead as an opportunity to serve and, in doing so, pushed the envelope for the men who stood shoulder to shoulder with me. Even as a young officer I was driven, decisive, and unwavering in my leadership approach. I allowed early life experiences to shape my perspective and in doing so found myself with a unique ability to identify with people from every walk of life. I could be off-color one minute and leading men outside the wire with dogged determination the next. Thinking outside the box wasn't always appreciated by senior leadership, but my desire to create and innovate encouraged me to push military cultural boundaries. Our community had become the first line of defense in the decades-long war on terror and because of it, we believed it solidified our place in history. From my perspective, however, we couldn't rest on our laurels. We weren't entitled to continued success because of the twenty years behind us. The world was quickly changing, and the Explosive Ordnance Disposal community had no choice but to keep pace in order to remain relevant. I was proud of our reputation as quiet professionals, but I also understood that for the sake of recruitment and budgeting, we had to ensure our position because we faced new threats coming out of China and Russia. This meant diversifying and expanding our skill set to stay ahead of technological advances. This kind of thinking isn't always popular. In time, as I became comfortable in my own skin, resting in my convictions was easier than conforming. I would have to choose whether I wanted the approval of others or the satisfaction of knowing I did what was right.

Somewhere along the way, I learned the importance of humility and personal accountability. Without it, it was tempting to forget that I hadn't gotten where I was on my own. Anyone who doesn't believe rank can't have that effect on a person isn't being honest. To disregard my own human nature would be the epitome of arrogance, and it's something many of us, including myself, are prone to in a field where we chase adrenaline and accolades. To combat this, as I became a senior officer, I purposely surrounded myself with men who trusted me enough to tell me when I was wrong. They knew my personal ethos and held me to the same standard I expected from others without compromise or apology. And it wasn't always easy. To have someone shut the door and tell me I was wrong because there were second or third order effects I hadn't anticipated meant humbling myself to the reality that I did not always have the right answers. When I took command of the Naval Dive and Salvage Training Center, one of my first orders was to distribute and post my command philosophy. It was imperative that every Sailor, Soldier, Airman, Marine, and Coastguardsman who passed through our doors understood the value of humility and accountability. I interviewed each new instructor who reported to the Command and made it clear that they had an obligation and duty to come to me if I was failing to uphold my oath of office. My Command Master Chiefs and Executive Officers received Letters of Instruction (LOI), signed and filed for the record, charging them with the duty to hold me accountable. Because if I failed, the entire Command suffered. So seriously did I take this responsibility, I empowered them to act on behalf of the Command if I was derelict in my duties. I lived through the devastation of a failed Commanding Officer, and I would not pave the same path to hell with good intentions. The damage of failed leadership due to one arrogant, entitled individual not only ruins careers, but it also inflicts invisible, personal wounds. I watched men struggle for years, doubting their own ability to thrive and succeed in the shadow of a poor Command climate and abuse of power. Failed leadership weakens institutions built on strength and accountability, undermining the core principles of service and sacrifice. We have an obligation to fortify ourselves against a misguided sense of entitlement in every element of our lives in order to maintain integrity, accountability, and decency. This was a principle I took seriously in the military and still carry with me today.

I believe a personal sense of entitlement is a thief. It robs a person of the desire to sacrifice and reason logically. It steals motivation and has revealed itself in the ugliest behavior we've witnessed in decades. It's hard to imagine what goes through a person's mind when they feel entitled, with eyes bulging and veins straining with the force of their rage, to scream obscenities in the face of the person opposite them just because they hold opposing views. We all witnessed entitlement manifesting itself when well-organized mobs descended on cities across the country, justifying their looting and rioting as they hurled bricks through store windows and lit entire city blocks on fire. During the summer of 2020, thousands of Americans believed they had the right to burn dreams and livelihoods to the ground, killing and maiming innocent men and women while causing over $1 billion in damages. Their anger was not righteous. It was fueled by a misplaced and misguided sense of entitlement, which continues to plague our streets. As cities turn into war zones and open-air drug markets and the news reports daily mass looting across the nation, we can only hope that the tide turns before some of our most beautiful cities are lost to a misguided social-political agenda. When American cities resemble third-world countries, we know we're losing the battle for the soul of our nation. To see hundreds of teenagers in Chicago destroy property or thieves brazenly rob supermarkets without legal recourse is a travesty. This inflated, misguided sense of entitlement has young men and women believing they are owed things they have not earned, leading to the ruination of entire communities. Shockingly, the wave of terror spreading across the nation is now supported by a justice system that has turned its back on their constituents in the name of social justice. Entitlement has become a new standard for adjudicating bad or illegal behavior, forcing residents in many communities to flee their history, homes, and dreams before becoming inevitable victims of crime.

If you're anything like me, you watch the news every day and are confounded by the lack of integrity and honesty in the legal system. It's obvious that crimes harshly punished are crimes not likely repeated. But we are now witnessing a two-tiered system of justice, where some Americans are entitled to certain privileges under the law that are not equally applied to others. Let's go back to the riots of 2020. Americans were consistently treated to a buffet word salad to explain away the daily destruction play out on national new networks. While TV screens flashed footage of businesses engulfed in flames, commentators robotically repeated the phrase "peaceful protests." Most of us were confounded, asking ourselves how this was allowed to continue. How many times would looters be allowed to break windows, disrupt traffic, threaten drivers, vandalize moving vehicles, and steal shopping carts of merchandise while police officers were targeted, assaulted, and in some cases, murdered? I think it's quite easy to explain. Those who participated had been led to believe they were entitled to a get-out-of-jail-free card. And it seems they were right. Surprisingly, lawyers were already waiting in the shadows to represent them. Even Kamala Harris encouraged her supporters on social media to donate monetarily to the Minnesota Freedom Fund to assist those arrested, regardless of the type of crime, with bail money. While everyone is innocent until proven guilty, there must also be a consensus from those in power that the law should be applied without public pressure or political interference. Instead of maintaining objectivity, especially as the violence played out publicly, elected leaders on the Left pursued an agenda meant to feed an ugly, divisive narrative. They made it clear that those who participated deserved an outlet for their anger and that justice was served with every brick thrown through plate glass and every person beaten for trying to defend their property. You cannot condemn violence but simultaneously support the perpetrators in both word and deed. That summer changed our justice system, and Americans must contend with the reality that victimization is an acceptable norm as long as the perpetrators are supported by weak, ineffectual district attorneys.

I am astounded at the overarching attitude of entitlement we're experiencing in our country, and it goes deeper than the crime touching almost every community whether rural or urban. I see the evidence of it in our military, and I see it in industry, although the consequences are quite different. We are living in a time when many among us believe they deserve privileges, services, or accommodations without having earned them. The belief that there should be nothing paid for what is historically earned has created fissures and cracks in basic socioeconomic relationships, now magnified and exacerbated by rising inflation and the staggering rise of consumer goods. At some point, everyone wanting something for free will become unsustainable, and we will have no one to blame but ourselves. Instead of practicing fiscal responsibility, our leadership remains more committed to the next election cycle than our economic strength or national security. Welfare, for example, is so politicized that streamlining programs, which statistically benefits both taxpayers and recipients long-term, becomes a biased talking point instead of modeling solution-based outcomes. Politicians conflate their sense of entitlement with the distribution of an entitlement, purposely confusing voters and lending credibility to a one-sided, emotional argument that welfare programs should have unlimited funding unmoored from personal accountability. Politicians in Washington epitomize the entitlement mentality with their gross neglect of the basic principles of governance. They see themselves as benevolent rulers bestowing alms to the poor while they use their power to increase personal wealth. The trickle-down effect taints each level of government with elitism, leaving communities desperate for growth and opportunity instead of poverty in perpetuity. Rest assured, when leadership lives in the suburbs free from the reminders of government-sanctioned poverty, they've divorced themselves from the reality of their charge.

Now, lifelong politicians justify their subversion of the law for political purposes and personal gain. Once considered positions shrouded in dignity, elected leaders yell profanities at one another on the House floor, seemingly more interested in becoming the next big headline than doing their job as public servants. The elite in Washington disguise themselves as a voice of the people but shift and maneuver to brand themselves, shilling their wares while they capitalize on social media platforms. The flagrant sense of entitlement from our elected leaders is so audacious it's led to total distrust in government institutions, even those designed to assist the most unprivileged. It's no wonder Americans have given Congress such an abysmal approval rating. If Washington believes they deserve lifelong positions void of accountability, then their constituents will respond in kind. The common attitude of "rules for thee, but not for me" exemplifies the entitlement mentality and creates a crippling divide of haves and have-nots. We all experienced this during COVID when the government demonized the most fundamental principles of critical thinking. It cultivated an extreme subset of society who had no fear of reprisal and took to social media to scream at, vilify, and shame those who made personal choices based on their individual circumstances. We should never forget the families whose special-needs children were kicked off airplanes because they were medically unable to keep a mask over their nose and mouth. We should still fight to hold accountable those who felt entitled to make the decision prohibiting families from being with their loved ones as they died alone in nursing homes and hospitals. No human being in society that reveres liberty deserved to be told they were "nonessential." In my lifetime, I don't think I've seen our society fracture and compartmentalize itself at the hands of unelected bureaucrats the way it did in those first eighteen months of the pandemic. I believe history will not be kind, and we do well to learn from these harsh lessons so they will not be repeated.

Elementary through high school, I was regularly quizzed by my parents about tests and grades. If I seemed to be slipping, the onus was on me and me alone to fix it. It was my responsibility to approach my teachers and ask for extra instruction or request tutoring. There was no world in which my mom marched herself to the school and blamed the teacher for my poor performance. If the teacher sent home a note, Mom did not write back a scathing defense, and she certainly didn't offer excuses on my behalf. In fact, she made it clear that the problem would be remedied immediately, and I was expected to find a solution. There were very few do-overs and because of it, it incentivized accountability. Education, specifically, has created entitlement as its own subject. It's not a spoken lesson or one given life with words. Those responsible for shepherding children teach entitlement through actions or lack thereof. Instead of allowing students to receive the grade they've earned, schools have changed philosophy and enforcement. In counties across the nation, students are offered multiple opportunities to repeat assignments or are provided a minimum grade for classwork regardless of effort. Some school systems across the country have ditched letter grades altogether to increase self-esteem and promote equity. The thought being that a "do no harm" philosophy insulates students from emotional harm and incentivizes hard work. If it seems ridiculous it's because it is. Name a kid in your life who wouldn't take the easy road if the choice meant doing less for the same grade. Teachers are leaving the profession in droves, abandoning the job they once felt was a life-long calling. In addition to political pressure from administrators and school boards, the entitlement attitude from students and parents has made teaching unbearable. Parents have become increasingly hostile toward teachers when confronted with little Johnny's bad behavior. When students are unaccountable for their performance or behavior yet somehow manage to excel academically, it reinforces the concept that they are owed reward without effort. This lack of accountability, coupled with the rabid protection of social justice agendas, leaves teens unequipped to live in a challenging, diverse world.

I cannot stress more emphatically the disservice we do our children by excusing their bad behavior or expecting too little of them in an academic environment. No one ever rises to meet low expectations. The classroom should be a place where diversity of thought is not only encouraged but respected. Consider the differences in life experiences and challenges in just one high school classroom. Imagine if we taught our young people to apply those experiences and challenges to economics, history, arts, and science. What would a school day sound like if the skills of active listening and respectful speech were priorities? There should not be a student body hierarchy in which certain minority groups are elevated and celebrated above other students. This division not only causes strife and tension, but it also cements policies that elevate specific individuals as a protected class, despite those privileges having a tangible effect on their peers. School boards should not be picking winning and losing moral debates. They are not entitled to approve speech under the pretense of providing equitable protection. They know that entitlement can't survive when you apply empathy, so healthy discourse is discouraged. Any dissenting topic from the popular narrative is labeled hate speech, a completely emotional argument steeped in fallacy. Your child's speech in school is not allowed to make another child uncomfortable, which means that they are not entitled to their own opinion. They are only allowed to agree or shut up. Being uncomfortable is an important life skill, and instead of asking students to defend their positions in a healthy environment, we call them all sorts of names and require their obedient silence. We've not only demeaned the role discomfort plays in personal growth, but we're actively staunching critical thinking and respectful discourse. There's a priority of feelings over facts, and it's emotionally and intellectually stunting a generation of young people who should be at the forefront of science, technology, and engineering. They should be preparing to lead the free world in a dynamic period in history, but we're too focused on safe spaces and public shaming. It's created a weird hybrid of adults patiently waiting for a six-figure job while student loans go unpaid and small businesses shutter because they can't find people willing to do blue-collar work. How unfortunate for our country and how crippling for them to have been sold entitlement as a tool to navigate life. We must help them believe again that there is purpose and meaning for their lives. It is incumbent upon us to hold them to a standard they can be proud of, and in doing so, we give them the strength to face the challenges of tomorrow.

While it's easy to place the blame on the current generation, I reject the notion that our young adults are creatures of their own making. The temptation to identify an enemy in the fight for truth and justice has pitted generation against generation, leaving us more divided than I can remember in my lifetime. Instead of leading from a place of wisdom, we've demonized and criticized the kids we've raised and the communities we've cultivated. We fed the technology monster without prejudice while simultaneously checking out of the classroom, leaving them to live and learn outside our influence. There's plenty of blame to go around. Parents withdrew and allowed social media to fill social gaps, especially when the world shut down. Institutions of higher learning have been promoting Marxism, entitlement, and hypocrisy for decades, but we still happily send our kids to universities where professors are highly influential activists. It's a tough pill to swallow, but we can't change what we won't acknowledge. If we want a strong country, it begins at home and in schools. What we're seeing today is the result of thirty years of vilifying and repressing freedom of thought or expression outside a strict social justice construct. It's been years of parents playing defense for their children in school or sports instead of holding them personally accountable for their actions. When the young Soldier left my office and rejoined his family, I was told his mother was quite livid. Instead of recognizing that her adult son had acted in a manner unbecoming a Soldier, she ranted at my CMC that "maybe I should go back where I came from," along with other unfortunate language. I was happy to hear that the Soldier apologized for his mother's profanity and the tirade was quickly stopped by the CMC, but it serves as a reminder that behavior, no matter how subtle, is modeled. Too many want to believe this phenomenon happened overnight. That COVID lit the fuse of activist propaganda and gross entitlement. While that is partially true, extreme activism quietly began years ago when no one was paying attention. During my congressional campaign, I met school board members who served in Fairfax County, Virginia, in the 1990s. They recounted their frustration at trying to bring attention to the inclusion of critical race theory in high schools. To their dismay, most members were unwilling to participate in a conversation, even for the sake of clarification. The county was the best in education throughout the nation, and any dissent was unwelcome. I honestly believe we became so entitled in our own freedom we allowed seeds of extremism to be sown in the most vulnerable place, our children's classrooms, and we are reaping the consequences of that pervasive ideological fruit.

One of the greatest lessons I've learned through trial, error, and humility was that I didn't always have to have the right answer. My rank didn't qualify me as the smartest guy in the room, and not every solution is reached with 100 percent satisfaction. But wisdom, however, meant surrounding myself with people who had answers to the questions I didn't. I made it a priority to recognize the talents and expertise of the people around me so everyone, including myself and my men, benefited. One of the chronic failures of leadership is believing you must be the only voice in the room with the answer. We see this throughout industry and with our elected leaders. When an individual is unwilling to admit they don't have all the answers, the people around them lose. We all lose. We create an island unto ourselves where we appoint ourselves judge, jury, and executioner. This is how hubris breeds entitlement and entitlement, pride. It's dying on a hill of self-righteousness when the 80 percent solution not only meets the immediate need but also instills satisfaction and confidence in the people around you. I was grateful to learn this relatively young, but currently this lesson is being delayed for the sake of comfort and politics. So much of what we teach or emulate revolves around the notion of being the first or the only. As if biology or melanin entitles anyone to a job, position, or title. There is a pervasive, self-centered narrative guiding this generation. They don't get the job and their knee-jerk, feel-good response is "they don't deserve me." You get a poor performance review, and it's immediately the boss's fault, a coworker's fault, a bad year personally. Honest self-reflection is required for personal growth, but the default has become entitlement. Introspection is probably one of the most underutilized personal habits but requires a willingness to hold oneself accountable in the process. We must be willing to separate facts from emotion because while we're entitled to our feelings, we are not entitled to our own version of the facts.

I talk a lot about failure because it's how I learned the most impactful lessons of my life. They shaped me instead of defining me, and because of them I have a perspective that has successfully carried me through the trials and tribulations of life. Like the young man who stood in my office at attention, hoping he hadn't forfeited months of training because of a false sense of entitlement, I too was given the opportunity to fail and try again. But I had to earn it. I was held accountable for my actions, took responsibility when I screwed up, and accepted that the outcome might not turn out the way I wanted despite my best efforts. It is good to put into practice accountability as a natural antidote for entitlement. Whether it's in the home, at our jobs, or even performing our civic duty, accountability rights a multitude of generational wrongs. It's why I advocate fiercely for people to vote. We have no right to complain about the mess in DC but stay home on election day; that is its own reckless vehicle for entitlement. It is not incumbent on our neighbors to vote us out of the failed policies we all suffer under. It is not someone else's responsibility to show up in November and cast a ballot while the world around them pretends they're too busy to engage. We must resist the temptation to divorce ourselves from the reality that not only does every vote matter but every vote is cast with the knowledge that the power is in the addition not the subtraction. Every time one person recuses themselves from the process, they knowingly withhold power from the people who do show up. We've become so numb to the constant bombardment of noise on our screens that we don't realize most of what we hear lacks depth or nuance. Every argument is steeped in emotion, and it keeps those who cling to entitlement like a badge of honor committed to their cause out of nothing but fear. This emotion-driven political commentary is what keeps the Left in business and winning elections. We must be cautious not to become what we loathe out of convenience or apathy. We must show up until there is nothing left to fight for.

No one owes us anything. We are endowed by our Creator to life, liberty, and the pursuit of happiness. Whether you were born here or came as an immigrant, the only promise this country makes is the guarantee of those three pursuits. The rest has to be earned by sheer will and determination. There will be countless opportunities, but the stark reality is that success or wealth is never guaranteed. I am grateful my family invested their time and attention in my education. It wasn't easy being held to a standard many of my peers were not, but I see now how it laid a foundation of accountability I could build on. It didn't feel good at the time, but my mom wasn't interested in the emotional arguments I used to plead for leniency. Her perspective of sacrifice was magnified by the understanding that education unequivocally leads to freedom. I was not allowed to wallow in my own immaturity because excellence, not entitlement, was the rule in our home and my school. It only takes one generation to change the course of human history. What we're faced with today can be undone, but only if we're committed. It doesn't mean returning to the past either. Too many wish for the days of yesteryear without acknowledging the immeasurable benefits of progress. Our commission is not to go backward; it is to move forward with unwavering resolve to uphold the principles that have defined our country for over two hundred and fifty years. Changing course will take time, but I have seen the generosity of the American spirit and it is still like no other in the world. But we will have to fight because there are those in power who want to destroy it. We are no longer entitled to quietly sit back and allow others to do the hard work. Our place isn't to assume someone else will stand in the gap for what is right or lead the charge to regain integrity and common sense in the process. The time for excuses or emotion is over. Our children need us to engage and sacrifice for the future of our nation because if America falls, there's nowhere else to turn.

HOW AMERICA FAILS

was hungry, tired, and angry. I could take the abuse, but doing it on an empty stomach was a particular kind of insult. It had been several days of sitting silently during lunch, berated by my upperclassman while the Midshipmen around me quickly devoured their food. This Second Class seemed to take extra pleasure in making an example of me in front of my classmates. As Plebes, we were required to read and be ready to be quizzed on two front page news items and one sports article as well as a host of other topics. Along with memorizing each daily meal menu, scheduled activities, and Navy rules and regulations, our capacity to think independently for our first year was purposely limited. We were at the mercy of our upper class, and it was always in our best interest to take the insults as they came. Unfortunately, I couldn't read enough articles to prepare me to speak intelligently about football, baseball, or really any sport that consumed Joe's heart and mind. An avid athlete who believed America's favorite pastimes defined the soul of a man, Joe was obsessed. My primary interests were martial arts and gymnastics, but Joe dismissed them at hand and insisted I choose football articles, grilling me on plays, teams, and statistics that not only did I have little knowledge of but that I held very little interest for. I think he found what he believed was a weakness in me and made it his mission to root it out. Then, when I began to struggle academically, I wasn't willing to spend precious time in the library learning the ins and outs of football while barely passing my classes. Day after day, I sat at attention with eyes forward, stomach groaning, while Joe explained why I wasn't fit to be an officer. According to him, I wouldn't know how to relate to or act around my fellow officers once I hit the Fleet. It didn't feel good. As Plebes, we all knew our lowly place in the Brigade and did our best not to stand out. They were tearing us down in order to build us back up; but, day after day, this felt personal. According to Joe, my naval career hadn't even started, and I was well on my way to becoming a failure. His one summer cruise and a lifetime of football games with his dad clearly made a lasting impression on him. But he had no more concept of the big Navy than I did. Joe was convinced he held the secret to becoming an outstanding naval officer and, in no uncertain terms, told me I was not the kind of American the country needed. I didn't represent what he thought a red-blooded American should be. But I kept my mouth shut, staring straight ahead, promising myself I'd prove him wrong. What Joe didn't understand at the time was I, and immigrants like me, would be exactly the kind of American this country needed.

Joe wasn't wrong about everything. I didn't know an intentional grounding or sack from my elbow. But it only took weeks into my first year to understand Navy football was a big deal. I learned to love cheering in the stands just as much as the time-honored tradition of stomping away the frigid cold during Army-Navy games in December. Parades before home games, the long march back to the Yard after hours of standing, tailgates, and pranks weren't about stats and plays. It wasn't even always about winning. It was seeing a big wave of black coats and white covers on the jumbo screen, not one Midshipman distinguishable from another. We sang our alma mater with one deafening voice in victory and defeat. We complained about the drills and parades, the constant orders to hurry-up-and-wait. Our time at Annapolis wasn't about having a college experience or figuring out who we were. We were Navy blue and gold, already hungry for a mission but holding space until we'd earned our place in the Fleet. Much like the student body at Thomas Jefferson, we came from all walks of life. There were sons of admirals and daughters of generals. A few kids had never seen the ocean, and there were plenty who hadn't traveled outside their home state. Some had family whose service went back generations, and others wanted to be the first to blaze a path of service in the armed forces. My best friends grew up in inner-city Richmond and sunny Southern California, respectively. Back then we didn't know the trouble ahead. We had no inkling of the insanity we'd be faced with or the overwhelming feeling that every corner of the world was on fire. Looking back, I see how our sweet spot in history gave us a false sense of bravado, but I think the naivete was a necessary precursor for what was to come. We had to have the tenacity to believe we were the best first, and the rest would follow.

Men and women like me, immigrants, refugees, and first-generation Americans, are a symbol of hope to a wayward nation. And we *are* a wayward nation, although I don't think most Americans want to believe we're a nation in decline. I get it. In the shadow of freedom, it's easy to ignore reality until it finally knocks on your own front door. Pornography in schools is easy to ignore when your kids are grown and flown. Never mind your tax dollars supporting the politization of government-run schools or the insidious sexual-identity indoctrination of kindergartners. We are certainly a people well-adapted to freedom in a way that's made us sluggish, almost criminally so, in our recognition of injustice, especially when it comes to the acceptable abuse of children. But the enormity of this truth either becomes a catalyst or the continuation of willful intellectual ignorance. In a time when there's brazen hostility toward learning and access to a wide variety of information, those who want to fundamentally transform the country are counting on our ignorance. If enough of us don't keep speaking and fighting for the truth, history will have no mercy on our generation. Today's young children are tomorrow's leaders, and they will hold us accountable for our selective engagement during a time of great upheaval. So far have we strayed from the fundamental principles of liberty that we've forgotten our duty to cherish and protect the future for those who will live long after us. Our comfort has created a passivity that encourages us to abandon hard truths instead of running toward them, and now the race is on to undo what has already been deceptively solidified in the hearts and minds of our young people.

A complacent, compliant nation bowed to the whims of radicalism cannot sustain itself. If America is to survive, and I'm not being hyperbolic when I say this, there must first be an overwhelming recognition of what is at stake. It's not enough to want change. We must be doers and seekers of the truth to combat the damaging narrative playing on repeat in the background of our daily lives. If you're anything like me, you've gotten to the point where you shake your head and wonder if this is the same America you grew up in. Is this really the land of the free and home of the brave? Did we ever think there would be a time when we would spend most of our waking days listening, debating, or being subliminally preached to about sexuality? At every turn, the ugliness is highlighted by the media and punctuated by politicians who use tragedy to stoke the flames of discord. It's like they're creating the fracture just to become the healers. In psychological terms I believe that's considered a mental illness, but in politics all's fair in an election cycle. But it's not enough to be outraged or astounded. It's not enough to shake our fist at the nightly news or boycott a woke corporation. Gone are the days when we could afford to be reactive. We must become offensive, already so engaged in every aspect of community that the ideology cannot take root in the first place. We've already allowed propogandists to control the narrative and untwisting the vines of deception seems impossible, but I don't believe it is. I just think it hasn't gotten bad enough for the general public to force them to engage in solutions. We are so prosperous, even by poverty-level standards, that our comfort has become a prison of our own making. If you dissect and consider the reasons why you choose not to speak up against the radical ideology seeping into every aspect of life, my suspicion is that the answer lies in fear. Fear of being uncomfortable, fear of losing control, fear of being disliked or judged. So we sit in safety and comfort, ignoring the reality that our neighbor's indoctrinated children will join the legal and education system with disproportionately un-American values and philosophies while your children fight the battles you ignored.

I've been to over forty countries in the world and have lived on several different continents. It has given me deep insight into humanity, especially when it comes to culture, tradition, and religion. Right now, America seems to be one of few countries willingly burning itself to the ground from the inside out. I've never seen anything like it in my lifetime. I've experienced war and lived in countries where banana republics and unrest are the norm. But even that precariousness is, unfortunately, baked into the culture. Most of the time, strife and violence have outside influences or oppressors. What we're experiencing in real time is the hasty decay of a free society from within, and we must ask ourselves why we allow it. Selfishly, I believe we're content as long as our wallets and self-interests seem protected. Apathy has become the overarching American sentiment. Commentators wonder out loud when the prevailing winds will finally shift, and America wakes up to the reality that we're quickly losing our national identity. But I think they're asking the wrong question. What we should be asking is how bad does it need to get before we finally say enough is enough? My fear is that by the time enough Americans finally arrive at this conclusion we will be too far down the blighted path of socialism. We will have forfeited freedom in inches only to be confronted by the realization that those inches cut a mile deep into our unalienable rights. The immigration crisis is a perfect example. The decimation of our southern border is so dire the number of illegal aliens who have flooded the streets of the US has surpassed the total population of fifteen states combined. And yet there is very little public outrage. No marches on Washington for our sovereignty, safety, and security. No candlelight vigils for the victims of overdoses, homicides, kidnappings, rapes, or trafficking at the hands of illegal aliens and a robust, violent cartel network. No politicians on the Left demanding justice or accountability for the 85,000 missing, and presumably exploited, children who have been tragically lost in a broken system of political bureaucracy. No outcry from every governor in the union in support and defense of their neighbor below them, demanding action in solidarity because we are one United States. Instead, the world watches as we pick each other apart, exploiting every real and perceived vulnerability including our borders, technology, and culture. Our decline is manifested in the lack of reverence for the rule of law, and we can't even agree on the method in which we protect our sovereignty. And although the solution is ridiculously easy to most logical people, the issue is now compounded a millionfold with innocent Americans left to deal with the fallout of a disastrous national security policy.

When I'm asked about immigration, as a refugee and natural-ized citizen, my response has been and will always be the same: you cannot expect the American dream if you do not follow American law. When my family came to the States, we did so legally and waited in line for citizenship along with thousands of others from all over the world. It couldn't have been easy for my parents to fill out and maintain mountains of paperwork for all of us. Green cards, work and school visas. It must have seemed insurmountable, the nav-igation of the immigration and naturalization process, especially with language and economic barriers. But they did it. We all waited our turn until the day we became citizens of the United States of America, and it was a moment I will never forget. Those of us who wait and toil, struggling through the red tape and seemingly end-less bureaucracy, have a greater appreciation of the sacrifice when we finally raise our right hand to swear our oath. Maybe you can appreciate it the same way if you've crossed the Rio Grande in the heat of summer and slipped through a barbed wire fence. Maybe. But I contend the process reveals motivation and motivation reveals long-term intent. I understand the desperation; our family lived it. But what we're seeing at the southern border isn't the same, and we should take care to remember that.

There can be no logical justification for the invasion at our southern border other than this Administration's hope of solidi-fying a particular voter base. The current Administration has pri-oritized poverty, crime, and disease over US law and citizenship in ways we have never experienced in this country. There has been no accounting for the economic detriment as taxpayers pour billions of dollars into housing, feeding, and transporting millions of illegal aliens across the nation. Border towns are overrun, their emergency rooms no longer quickly or reasonably accessible to residents. The surge in illegal immigrants needing health care has all but drained community resources in towns along the entire southwest, leaving residents out of options. States of emergency have forced hospitals to hire additional staff at their own expense with illegal immigrants receiving free medical care that is not offered to legal residents. Not only is health care collapsing at the border, but all over the United States, schools are beyond capacity and without the resources to handle the influx of immigrant children. From north to south, east to west, cities across the nation find themselves without direction or guidance from the federal government on how to keep up with the demand of illegal immigrants flooding their streets. For those that purported themselves to be sanctuary cities and welcomed the slow trickle of illegals over the course of the past twenty or thirty years, I say this is a disaster of their own making. To buck federal law in order to virtue signal has finally reaped its consequences, and I feel very little empathy for the crocodile tears that accompany each new press conference from progressive leadership. How easy for them to extol their liberal virtues when it suited them politically but now that their policies have come home to roost, they wail over their plight. Elections have consequences, and the border crisis has been a profound example of this very fact.

There's another piece of this border crisis puzzle very few are willing to talk about. Maybe it's not considered politically expedient, but I'm willing to wade into the deep end of a hard conversation because avoidance does nothing when solutions are required. For too long, we have overlooked the complex but necessary attribute of assimilation in any conversation surrounding immigration. It is a reasonable and sound expectation that anyone seeking the American dream must also be willing to embrace the language and culture of their new home. Not only for our sake but for theirs. That doesn't mean a forfeiture of their native culture but prioritizing the steps to becoming a productive member of the very society they asked to join. That means actively learning the language and learning the laws of the land. It means not expecting this country to adapt to them but for them to want to adapt to this country. For example, when we were stationed in Naples, Italy, my wife, son, and I did whatever we could to assimilate to our surroundings. While we obviously weren't seeking citizenship, we still had an obligation to respect our place as guests in our host nation and do our best to adapt. The first step was educating ourselves about the customs and culture while actively engaging to learn the language. Yes, it was quite different and could be frustrating, especially trying to work on the Italian timetable, but it was not our right to dictate an American way of living to an entire nation of people who had their own habits and customs. It was our responsibility to adapt to them, not expect them to adapt to us. I think it was a surprise to many Americans stationed there that most Italians did not speak English. Having lived and worked overseas during much of my life, I didn't find it unusual. But there were families unaware of how much they would need to assimilate if they wanted to thrive during their time in Europe. For us, it was an incredible added value to be able to assimilate and learn the customs and culture of a beautiful country with wonderful people. Not only did it provide us with one more opportunity to stretch ourselves personally, but eventually it made coming home all the sweeter.

In a culture that now promotes equity as a utopian American trait, assimilation is projected as demonizing and demoralizing to the immigrant. I disagree. As a legal immigrant, I understood and appreciated the importance of adopting American values. Even as a young boy, I was smart enough to realize it didn't mean a complete abandonment of my native language and culture. But if my parents wanted us to be here so desperately, then it was worth the struggle to learn the language and adopt the spirit of what it meant to be an American. It wasn't easy, but it was necessary. Coming here, by whatever means and for whatever reason, is ultimately a choice. When I see military-aged men sneaking by night into the country, carrying lethargic children drugged to keep them quiet, I must ask myself if they're coming here to be a part of us. Are they here to help continue the American dream for the next person or to ransom it like a thief for their own benefit? The women and girls who make it here smuggled by coyotes or cartels, raped and tortured along the way, separated from their family and children, what will their role be? The evidence of their terror hangs on a tree in the Arizona desert; undergarments both small and large twisted around branches to flaunt unrestrained lawlessness on American soil. Broken and traumatized, used and forgotten, what will these women think of the country that not only allowed it to happen but encouraged it? Barely raised a hand to stop it. I can only imagine how their nightmare will quietly transform our culture in the years to come. How do you not loathe the very people who gave evil the freedom to terrorize and exploit? There is no scenario in which the millions of illegal aliens now sleeping on American streets or in overcrowded, makeshift shelters adopt an attitude of appreciation that later translates into loyalty. What they believed would be a dream has devolved into hopeless resignation. They were told America was open for business because every means to stop them from coming was eliminated. They received phones, gift cards, and transportation to a city far away from the border only to realize, ultimately, there was no place for them to go. No house waiting for them. No family to take them in, no place to call home. No purpose or goal other than their next meal or shower. Court dates five to ten years in the future with nothing in between. They assumed jobs and opportunity would be waiting. Why else would we make it so damn easy for them to come? If we don't grasp the multigenerational backlash we'll experience over this folly, then shame on us for our own lack of foresight.

I don't understand the people who protest physical walls or bemoan the importance of technological surveillance as a tool in our national security arsenal. The federal government has a duty and obligation to vet any person wanting to live and work in our country, and the reasons for doing so are multifold. First, priority should be given to those who are experiencing life-threatening political or religious persecution in their native country with the presumption that political affiliation and religious beliefs are often comingled. We are nothing if not a bastion of freedom for those who want to worship or practice their faith without fear of imprisonment or death. Second, we must be assured that the majority coming here for work visas have skills that add value to our communities and industries at large. We should place high value on tradesmen, technical workers, and entrepreneurs. The Vietnamese American community is the perfect example of a strong, resilient immigrant population who wasted no time assimilating and capitalizing on the American dream. For over forty-five years, oftentimes despite traumatic and treacherous beginnings, Vietnamese Americans have demonstrated a work ethic and ingenuity that has made them successful across the nation. They are respected in their communities and silent professionals who, until the 2016 election, did very little to garner public attention. Lastly, we must ensure those coming here do not pose a risk to any American. That risk may be physical, but it may very well be economic. There is no doubt crime and drug use increase with illegal immigration. In fact, what Joe Biden continues to do by releasing illegal immigrants instead of returning them to their country of origin is grant mass parole. Think about that. We don't know who they are or what they've done, yet they've been allowed unfettered access to our communities. Despite the government's actions to the contrary, there is no such thing as unlimited resources. When vital services have been stretched beyond their capacity to effectively support a community, state, or country, then the cause must be addressed and remedied immediately. This should not be a partisan issue. The rule of law and welfare of Americans must be the priority if we are to continue as a civilized society.

Immigrants know better than most the sacrifice it takes to start a new life. Our voice is one of common sense and dignity and continues to resonate, even during discord, with the American people. We recognize the importance of waiting our turn, no matter how long and how difficult the journey. It doesn't mean it's easy, especially for those living in fear. But we see now the alternative, and those who are desperately waiting in line will have to wait longer. Their fate precariously hinged on the speed of an already fatigued and ineffective immigration system all because they chose to follow the law of the land. They don't just want to live here; they want to be Americans. There can be no doubt that the man-made crisis at our southern border puts lives in danger both here and abroad. We are supposed to be a compassionate nation. What we're not doing at the border, our careless lack of action, is far from compassionate. We are aiding in the trafficking of women and children. Dangerous men have created a commodity-focused business in smuggling human beings, yet we sit back and allow them to come. Our border patrol is long past its breaking point with no promise of relief, and our resources are utterly depleted. We have no means to account for everyone who has requested asylum and been transported to major cities across the country. Think about the role of our federal government for a moment and then consider its lack of intuitive progress to streamline any process that requires authentication, investigation, or follow-up. The backlog, the red tape. We've all experienced it in one way or another. Our veterans can't get the mental health care they need because there aren't enough resources to provide the care or efficiently authorize timely treatment. But somehow the federal government can magically handle an influx of almost eight million people and counting who will now have to traverse the legal, health, and welfare system parallel to American citizens. It's ludicrous. We've sacrificed the country's security on the altar of politics, and believe me when I tell you there are no other reasons for this travesty outside of political power.

Many people want to make this an "us against them" argument. Like the people seeking asylum are somehow subhuman or undeserving of becoming Americans. Beware. It's emotional blackmail politicians and special interest groups use to evoke sympathy during an election cycle and should be completely discounted because it has no basis in fact or reality. There is a reason, a good one, that so many want to come to this amazing nation and take advantage of the wealth and opportunities available for those willing to work hard. It's the reason my family, and millions like mine, came legally over the years and made a life for themselves. And notice what is ignored by the media. It is not an accident that the illogical and divisive rhetoric of systemic racism has had no effect on the number of brown and black people risking their lives to come here. This fallacy, predicated on progressive, Marxist ideology, hasn't stopped Africans, South Americans, or Asians from pouring over our southern border in droves because even across the world they handedly separate fact from fiction. I don't blame them for their desire to live here, but we cannot be an economic sanctuary for the entire world. We must stop apologizing for wanting to prioritize resources. We must never capitulate when it comes to taking care of US citizens first so we can pursue legal, compassionate changes to immigration law if that is what Americans believe should be a priority.

The bigger picture here rests solely on the consequences of maintaining the status quo from the past several years. Given our social frailty, rampant crime, staggering national debt, increasing inflation, unsustainable illegal immigration, war and rumors of war, it pains me to consider the possibility of the greatest experiment in human history finally coming to an end. Historians have documented their failures through the ages, and if history has taught us anything, we either learn from it or we go the same way. I don't think it's unreasonable to assume it can't happen here, but there's still enough arrogance keeping us from acknowledging the truth. The same arrogance that allows our comfort to dictate our actions blinds us to the reality of national decline, and there are people in Washington who are glad of it. They need us complacent, distracted, unmotivated. We're not quite ready to admit that change begins at home. Our wallets may be lighter, but we're not uncomfortable enough to vote differently or hold Washington accountable. The immigrants at the border are still a long way from sleeping outside our homes or businesses. We cling to partisan promises instead of acknowledging what our eyes can see. All of this while they wait patiently in our valley of apathy knowing their power will remain long after the last remnants of liberty have faded. This is how a country fails. And if America fails, the world will have nowhere to turn. Universities proudly revere the promises of socialism and the evils of capitalism while ignoring the swarms of people from all over the world willing to die just to step foot on our shores. Even those who have led the way of the social justice movement, painting middle class Americans as terrorists and fascists, refuse to leave. For all the people who believe we are a terrible, inhumane, despicable nation, the path through the southern border still only cuts one way. There is no mass exodus out of the United States. Americans aren't applying for asylum in other countries because the truth is that there is no other country on earth that offers more individual freedom and liberty. They may speak words of dissension, but notice how content they are to live under the umbrella of freedom created over two hundred years ago by the very men they claim were evil, racist, and oppressive. We do well to highlight the irony in our efforts to combat this insidious narrative.

Joe couldn't have known his words would have such a lasting impact on my life. Not only did they not dissuade me from my purpose, but his words steeled my resolve. Nothing would stop me from becoming an American my country could be proud of. I didn't believe his lies because at nineteen I had already lived the truth of the American dream. I had already seen the blessings that come with sacrificing everything for the people you love. I never learned to love football apart from Army-Navy games, and he was right, over my twenty-five-year career I didn't always fit in. I never drank or partied with the Team. My drink of choice was Coke, and I excused myself early to go home and tuck my kids in bed at night. I didn't hide behind a desk, and I never asked my men to do something I wasn't willing to do myself. My men didn't seem to care either way. What they needed was someone to fight for them, and I worked every day to be worthy of their loyalty and respect. And when it was finally time to say goodbye, to take off my uniform for the last time, I promised to continue to serve the country that so graciously gave my family a flag to fly under and a place to call home. If we are to face the challenges of tomorrow, we must acknowledge the reality of today. Refugees and immigrants like me are reminders that America, while she may have lost her shine, has not completely lost her way. Yet. She is still a nation worth fighting for, and I believe our stories will be the collective voice carrying us back to freedom. It is up to us to remind the American people that hardships are never insurmountable as long as freedom is still a part of the equation. It's also up to us to communicate a clear message that unequivocally denounces illegal immigration as one of our greatest threats to our national and economic security. We must not equivocate and pander to progressivism that boasts blanket rights for all without accountability or due process. It is incumbent on us to be stewards of the American dream, if not for our children then for the children who one day hope to come from faraway places and live in the shining city on a hill.

IF I WERE THE ENEMY

f I wanted to knock down a building without anyone noticing, I wouldn't use a bulldozer. I wouldn't use explosives or call in a demolition crew. Instead, I'd release termites to swarm, infiltrate, and gnaw away at the foundation. Then, I'd bide my time and patiently watch as it slowly crumbles, its occupants none the wiser. This is what I told the Under Secretary of Defense when I briefed her on our work in Sensitive Activities to weaken our adversaries abroad. For the three years I led this specialized division at the Defense Threat Reduction Agency (DTRA), we used every form of technology and ingenuity to support Special Operations Command. It was important to communicate to her the breadth of our mission, and this was the analogy I used to illustrate what we did and why it was necessary for the safety and security of our nation. It's not enough anymore to use drones and missiles. We must push the envelope of unconventional warfare to undermine and subvert the will of countries working tirelessly against our interests. Unbeknownst to most Americans, our only options in conflict aren't ground wars and diplomacy. Like other nations, most notably Russia and China, our intelligence agency and military understand the most effective threats are often internal. Capitalizing on that fact means causing strife between reluctant allies. Destabilization within factions doesn't guarantee their failure, but the ensuing discord can compromise their ability to organize and execute attacks both kinetic and cyber. Working in Sensitive Activities taught me that the building is never the target, it's the people inside. Those who have been swayed by a narrative and lulled into a false sense of security. They ignore the tiny piles of wood dust or fine cracks climbing from the corners, unwilling to investigate the foundation because they still feel safe within their four walls. The day the floor finally shifts and the ceiling collapses while its occupants are asleep in their beds, that is how wars are won. If done correctly, military deception, sabotage, and subversion are enough to bring down a nation. What I see happening over the past several years in the US is the result of organizations who have had the diligence and patience to play the long game. To undermine freedom one hashtag and culture crisis at a time in order to threaten society's recognition of tyranny and oppression.

If I were the enemy of America, I'd start slowly. Quietly. I would hide in plain sight. My methods would seem quite reasonable, laudable even in certain circles where wealth and influence trickle down like a stream instead of a river. At first, I'd use the system itself to promote ideologies that dare push beyond the acceptable narrative all within the comfort of the status quo. Just enough to make people feel uncomfortable without them feeling threatened—or at least hesitant enough to question without worrying about appearing unreasonable. Take affirmative action as an example of leveraging ingrained policies already solidified in several facets of society affecting everything from education to business. Instituted as a means to reverse and correct injustice, the argument can be made that affirmative action had its place in society following the Civil Rights Act of 1964. Especially in areas of the country slow to respond to the new law honoring the rights of all Americans regardless of race, religion, sex, or national origin. Its goal was to bridge gaps in employment and education for minorities who had previously suffered under legal discrimination. But as time passed and progress swept the whole of society, affirmative action became a mainstay and, later, a subtle springboard for the Left's diversity, equity, and inclusion propaganda. If society could accept the notion that merit was secondary to race, sex, or skin color, then the possibility of mainstreaming ideologies like critical race theory and DEI were not only a reality but a certainty. As history has shown time and time again, any endeavor to elevate qualities like skin color, race, religion, or sex means disqualifying a counterpart based on the same. Using injustice to advance injustice has become a founding principle in racially motivated activism.

Using qualities that are unchangeable as a means of defining outcomes not only redefines success, it also eventually perpetuates what many refer to as the "bigotry of low expectations." If race or color supersedes experience and expertise, then the message we've silently communicated over the past forty years is the necessity of meeting a quota over the value of competition and merit. It's no longer who's the best for the job or the university but who first checks the most appropriate box; who appeases donors and the deep pockets of special interest groups. The concerns of having underqualified or ill-equipped students and workers in environments they may be unprepared for has long fallen on deaf ears. To question affirmative action's relevance in the modern era is to somehow suggest a return to bigotry, and so we continue even though cracks began to show in our foundation. On a micro scale, there are indications we've set young people up for failure by placing them in environments they may not be prepared to excel. There have been longstanding concerns about students being offered admissions placement to schools they're unprepared for academically but are accepted based on their minority status. All of this while simultaneously excluding qualified students who no longer receive preferential minority status because they consistently demonstrate high performance academically. On a macro scale you had a presidential candidate boasting his running mate for vice president would be either a person of color or a woman. The qualifications were secondary, identifiable traits primary. Racial preference continues to divide, manifesting in distrust among Americans within workplaces and institutions of higher learning. That, compounded by the astounding idiocy of critical race theory, has only deepened divisions where they hadn't previously existed. If I were the enemy, I would capitalize on the ways we continue to categorize people while simultaneously encouraging a victim mindset that inherently pits "us against them." Persuading people that their race or sex guarantees their failure ensures we lose our commonality, which is imperative to the activist objective: to create a distrustful and broken society unable to find common ground or moral clarity.

If I were the enemy, I would emotionally separate parents from children for eight hours a day. I would designate classrooms as a "safe space," which teaches secrets and code words only to be shared in class and not at home. I would seek out children who are vulnerable or curious and encourage that curiosity by depositing favor and attention the same way I'd feed a piggy bank: one affirmation at a time. Separating children from parents is the single most impactful tool in the Marxist playbook as it seeks to make the State the primary parent in the nuclear family. If a child is led to believe they can't trust their parents, the most likely default adult will become the teacher who spends the majority of the day using their influence in either a positive or negative way. Parents should be the adjudicators of what and who are influencing their children, but school boards across the country haven't just blurred the lines but erased the sanctity of the parent-child relationship. We know why they're doing it because they've said it long enough and loud enough for there to be no confusion. They're pushing an ideological agenda that is in direct conflict with anything morally grounded in faith or truth, and they have no intention of stopping.

During the midterm election, I went to several local high schools during football games and stood outside to give parents and students an opportunity to ask questions about any of my positions or proposed policies. One person stood out, and I will remember what she told me for a long time to come. She wasn't a young teacher with colored hair and a rainbow T-shirt. She was mid-to-late fifties, dressed conservatively, with an open smile and proud of being a public high school teacher of almost thirty years. I add this descriptor to make the point that too often we confuse appearance with ideology and make the mistake of underestimating the reach radical activism has in our schools. Her first question to me was direct, which I appreciated. Was I anti-teacher? Of course not, I told her. Teachers are underpaid and overworked as our family knows from numerous friends who have dedicated their lives to education. They are a blessing to our communities, but as we've seen over the last several years, their influence can also be a hurt if there is a hidden agenda. As the conversation progressed and I had a chance to ask my own questions, this teacher frankly and honestly dismissed the idea that parents should be included in any decision having to do with gender identity. In fact, she went so far as to state that it was *her* job to keep students safe from parents who may abuse them if they want to identify differently than their assigned sex. You just never know what happens in a child's home, she said. Her words were adamant and fervent. I think she believed her dedication was admirable. But I saw her position as abuse of the unique trust given to her as an educator. She deemed herself fit to be mental health provider, physician, and parent to children without any thought of the long-term relational and physical consequences to the child. She believed her role as teacher gave her an authority that superseded that of a parent.

It was an eye-opening revelation to hear firsthand instead of reading it in a teacher's union handbook. Her motivation clear, she was unwavering in her belief that parents become abusers if their child expresses a desire to change their gender identity. Her confidence in a message unsubstantiated by facts, studies, or even anecdotal evidence just goes to show how far down the slippery slope we've descended. To her, and school systems like her, for a parent to merely disagree with or make the decision against allowing a child to socially transition is tantamount to abuse. And she is not alone in her beliefs. In Virginia, a state legislator proposed a bill that would make parents who deny their child "the right" to socially transition a crime warranting intervention from Child Protective Services and possibly law enforcement. We also see these devastating and immoral policies in California and Washington state. Empowering adults in charge of children, especially in early childhood education, to devise and manipulate the mind of a child is not only corruption, it is ethically abhorrent. It is grooming, and we see the results on college campuses as students go on to glorify segregation, anti-Semitism, and the medical castration of minors. If I were the enemy, I would rejoice at the majority of parents who still don't speak up or advocate for their children. We have over eighty thousand students in my home, Loudoun County, Virginia. Can you imagine if even half of their parents showed up to one school board meeting? Tens of thousands in one night advocating for their right to raise their children without ideological influence. Forty thousand parents pressuring their elected school board members every single meeting to focus on reading, writing, and arithmetic instead of social justice and racial politics.

If I were the enemy, I would foster a spirit of victimhood that distracts from the real purpose of education. I would make schools a safe haven for indoctrination and activism instead of holding students to a standard of excellence and mastery. I would teach them what to think, not how to think, impeding their ability to become productive members of society. Eventually, enough young men and women would become ill prepared and unwilling to take on the fiscal and intellectual challenges of adulthood, threatening a strong and robust national workforce. If I were the enemy, I would scoff at merit linked to academic achievement, and I would abolish valedictorians, honor roll, and Advanced Placement courses. I would make sure every child is held to the lowest standard of learning in order to maximize equity, satisfied with mediocrity as long as standardized testing keeps state and federal money flowing. Cell phones and TikTok would be the biggest distraction and influence in schools, and educators would feel helpless to uphold disciplinary actions for fear of legal reprisal from parents and administrators. Even now, as test scores reach their lowest levels in thirty years and school districts face entire student populations illiterate in both math and reading, there is little urgency for change. Parents are weary and unengaged or don't feel like their voice matters. Our only certainty is that a solution won't come from inaction. If I were the enemy that is what I'd continue to count on.

If I were the enemy, I would ensure Ivy League schools become a breeding ground for terrorist sympathizers, elitism, and radicalism. I would consider the metamorphosis from religious institutions to oppressive indoctrination machines a stunning success after hearing students chant and cheer for the beheading of children and the rape and execution of women. Watching white women waving the same flags carried by radical Muslim terrorists across the world would signal to me total indoctrination. On October 7, 2023, Israel was attacked by the terrorist organization Hamas, murdering over 1,300 people in some of the most barbaric and brutal examples of inhumanity the world has ever seen. Civilians, not the Israel Defense Forces, were the intended targets, and many were ambushed as they lay sleeping in their beds or were pulled from safe rooms before being shot, beheaded, or burned alive. Children, the elderly, and the severely handicapped were kidnapped and ten days later have yet to be recovered as the Middle East hovers on the brink of war. Ivy League campuses led the world in an outcry of support for Hamas and their heinous crimes and continue to do so unashamedly with complete confidence their schools will support their hate speech. If I were the enemy, witnessing the almost frenzied hate for the Jewish and Arab victims at the most prestigious institutions in the world would make this part of my mission complete. As a graduate from both Harvard and MIT fellowship programs, I am appalled but unfortunately not surprised by the discrimination and dangerous sentiments taught in higher education. As an adult and established leader in my field, I had no problem ignoring the blatant bias often presented during the course, deftly sifting through the information that would further my professional growth. But I can easily imagine the influence such extreme bias has on young minds who are susceptible to the very blatant and purposeful DEI agenda, which categorizes everyone as either "oppressed" or "oppressor." Their influence is entrenched in our consciousness as a society, and because of it they've become the lightning rod of corruption and ideological ruin of our children. We must immediately address, and no longer ignore, the rampant anti-Semitism and anti-faith instruction on college campuses. These students are the future leaders of the free world, men and women who will be sought after solely for the piece of paper they receive upon graduation, and they're actively sympathizing with Nazi leaders who led over six million Jews to their deaths. The pandemic of hate being tolerated and encouraged at Ivy League schools should be a wake-up call for parents, just as it's become a wake-up call for corporations that are now publicly (and rightfully) committing to not hiring graduates openly affirming genocide while calling for the death of the Jewish people. Diversity, equity, and inclusion policy is at the heart of the gross anti-Semitism and anti-Christian movement on campuses because both are deemed by the elite as "oppressors" and "colonizers." This trend of sponsored and endorsed hate, along with the indoctrination of students at top-tier schools, has been happening for decades, and it's time for it to end. Parents and donors have a moral obligation to withdraw their financial support so these institutions wither on the vine long enough for them to cease to be relevant in a humane and safe society.

If I were the enemy, I would confuse language and distort perceptions. I would convince the masses that a biological male can in fact become a biological female capable of menstruation and carrying a child. There would be no reasoning, your objections would be met with emotional manipulation, and if that didn't work, I would call you names publicly reserved for the worst of mankind. Names that don't align with the diversity, equity, and inclusion movement, and harken back to dark days in our nation's history. I would have the full support of every major corporation in America, having invested hundreds of millions of dollars in diversity policy and training. You would be branded, set apart by the mere implication of intolerance. Your reasoning, even backed by science, would become a scarlet letter for all to see. New language would be socially engineered gently and cunningly over a long period under the cover of justice with the singular purpose of weakening any resolve to fight back. If I were the enemy, I would convince a generation that speech can be synonymous with violence based solely on hurt feelings, and I would eradicate personal accountability. Everyone would get a trophy starting from age five, consequences would be deemed unkind or unfair, and children encouraged to believe they are more special and deserving of achievement or promotion than their peers. We would become a country so consumed with our own vanity and personal safety we'd refuse to put down our phones long enough to rescue a woman being raped on a subway or stop an elderly man from being beaten to death on his front lawn. If I were the enemy I would chip away at our humanity with every click, like, and sound bite.

If I were the enemy, I would undermine women's equality, putting them back in conflict with men for everything from awards to scholarships to titles. I'd create a hostile atmosphere forcing them to defend their right to privacy and equality, labeling them selfish or hysterical for having the audacity to express discomfort while undressing in front of a man or having a man undress and expose himself to them. I would shame them into silence by threatening their scholarships and future careers, and that shame would keep them from standing up for their own physical and mental welfare. I would hound them, gaslight them, persecute them, until they no longer trusted the instincts their mothers spent a lifetime instilling in them about safety, privacy, and decency. If I were the enemy, I would remind women they have no place in society unless it's given to them by a man, even if that six-foot-three man wears a dress, has facial hair, and uses his physical strength to rage at anyone who misgenders him. How quickly a society changes when half can be bullied into silence. I'm appalled we're at a place in history when a woman can't say she's uncomfortable, intimidated, or fearful without threat of retribution from men. We created a deranged solution for a problem we never had. My wife and I have taught our three daughters that they are the only ones who can decide what makes them comfortable. Not only is it not the right for anyone else to tell them what to think or feel, but it's certainly not the right of a man disguising himself as a woman to tell them they must comply, they must look, they must shut up, and they must endure. It's the exact same language abusers use to ensure their victims remain powerless. After fifty years of progress, girls and women are once again fighting for the right to advance in spaces dedicated to their safety and success. If I were the enemy, I would be thrilled so many mothers and grandmothers are remaining silent in the face of discrimination against their daughters and granddaughters. I would hail the chronic emasculation of men over the past two decades a triumphant success because their voices should be the loudest in defense of their mothers, daughters, and sisters. And yet there is overwhelming silence. As the enemy, I know corrupting the role of men and fathers will usher in victory because men who won't fight for the women in their lives certainly won't fight for their nation.

Forget about the recklessness of redefining a woman—if I were the enemy, I would twist and distort the definition of a child. By refusing to define life or acknowledge the personhood of children, it would be simple to exchange moral clarity for moral equivocation. I know a society that does not value life hangs precariously in the balance, their humanity an illusion. If I were the enemy, I would make this the rallying cry of an entitled, uneducated generation so easily persuaded they're willing to compromise values, common sense, and decency all for the sake of emotions. Manipulating young people to believe their feelings dictate facts will do more to advance the pro-abortion, anti-child, and anti-woman agenda than special interest money ever will. As a bonus, emotional manipulation will also create long-term barriers to learning while diminishing the ability to thoughtfully and subjectively analyze data. It fosters an atmosphere where there's an unwillingness to apply data to factually and logically seek solutions to problems most Americans believe should be a priority, like supporting women during pregnancy and improving maternal-fetal medicine in the United States. But emotional arguments ride the wave of sympathetic headlines and political talking points, and if I were the enemy, I would use them to coddle young minds by feeding them highlight reels on TikTok about the mythological sanctity of life. The arguments against life have become so convoluted they border on the obscene, but maybe that has always been the goal. To convince someone that a life has zero value one minute before leaving the womb but is considered a child the second it evacuates the womb is not anchored in reality or science. It is immoral and fraught with a chilling lack of common sense, yet this is a critical talking point when the personhood of a child is broached with pro-choice advocates and liberal lawmakers. The refusal to admit personhood or acknowledge life is not a question without an answer; in fact, biologists both atheist and evangelical freely admit life begins at the moment of conception. The refusal now to acknowledge the data is purely political and has not only drawn dividing lines with voters, it's also distracted from medical, ethical, and emotional issues facing both women and children during an incredibly vulnerable period of life.

If I were the enemy, I wouldn't just remove God from the public square, I would crucify His influence and relevance in the hearts and minds of all Americans. I would make God the enemy of humanity and free thought and the instigator of war and destruction. His word would be twisted in pulpits not only across the country but around the world to fit popular culture, distorting human nature until we're left unconstrained in deeds and words. Our moral bedrock would lack the direction of one of the most generous commandments: to love our neighbor as ourselves—an idea that should be embraced by all religions and by all humanity. If I were the enemy, my rhetoric would condemn the resolve of those who fight for religious freedom for all people, and I would bastardize Jefferson's letter to the Danbury Baptists for the generation who've already sacrificed wisdom for ideology. Religion would be replaced with secular humanism, which can only be fulfilled in political spaces, until society became fragmented and inhospitable. Self-control, grace, and mercy would be replaced by anger, violence, and contempt, all manifesting in the degradation of relationships among parents and children, family and friends. If I were the enemy, we would no longer be *imago Dei*, image bearers of God. We would be creations of our own design with no urge to reflect anything to the world other than compulsion and greed. There would be nothing kind left in us, and we would be ruled by forked tongues and calloused fingertips hell-bent on provocation instead of peace. Removing God isn't just a tool; it's a weapon formed against the bonds of human nature and Heaven itself.

Knowing your opponent is one thing, but knowing your enemy requires a level of sophistication and dedication only time can measure. The enemy understands most strengths can be used to target inherent weaknesses, and they've taken great care to exploit our uniquely American freedom of expression and speech. With the help of a compromised media and the capricious nature of social media, they use our freedom in real time to communicate their own messages of hate, violence, and oppression with little restriction. As the nation continues to experience the unyielding background noise of radical rhetoric, we're also beginning to hear collective whispers advocating for censorship and restriction of our fundamental right to free speech at every level of government and within institutions. But we must remember, free speech is crucial not just for the obvious issue of personal liberty and expression. It requires members of a free society to subject themselves to counter viewpoints and philosophies. Not only does it force us to be exposed to opinions that challenge us collectively and individually, traditionally it also protects us against the perils from weakness of character and intellect. Censorship, like what we're seeing today across the vastness of media platforms and in universities, doesn't simply contribute to a weakness of mind and spirit, it pours the gasoline while activist educators light the match. We now see daily the consequences: agitation, meltdowns, and violent propaganda from people who are too weak of mind to use reasoning and logic to be members of a healthy, functioning society. For some, this may be considered the slippery slope of free speech, but I believe it's better to know exactly who people tell you they are. Free speech exposes moral corruption and reveals the enemy's grotesque assault on freedom and personal liberty, giving us exactly what we need to fight back and win. While freedom of speech doesn't compromise, it should be revered as one of the most potent tools for change, and we must wield it responsibly, using its power to educate and unite a broken and volatile nation.

The enemy of freedom is also predictably unpredictable. Until they're not. To get into the mind of the enemy is to intentionally and strategically focus on the end result and work backward to identify the most effective mechanisms of destruction. On one of my last missions during active duty, two former Green Berets and I were asked to provide an immediate threat assessment at a base in Somalia that had been attacked by the terrorist group Al-Shabaab. The Baledogle Military Airfield, located ninety miles north of the Mogadishu, provided crucial air support for the war on terror and became a target for radical militants. There was no doubt another attack was imminent, and the four-star General, in a quest to get answers for the attack, requested a comprehensive threat assessment to pinpoint any potential catastrophic failures in security. The base had been constructed to resemble a base in the States and later fortified by engineers in the same way. But what worked at home wouldn't work in the hard red clay of Somalia, where it gummed up the automatic main gates after it rained. Although the main gate was considered the presumptive target, in the several days it took to do our assessment, our ability to see a possible attack from the terrorists' perspective concluded the main gate would not be the primary focus of an assault. We credited the engineers with digging a large trench around the airfield perimeter fence to stop vehicles delivering Improvised Explosive Devices, but we saw the probability of Al-Shabaab using the trench as cover or camouflage much more likely. We made our recommendation based on where we believed the true vulnerabilities were, what their intended target actually was, and what they would use to achieve that goal. We directed training to that end. Several months later, Al-Shabaab attacked Baledogle in the exact way we'd predicted during our assessment. With a few low-cost modifications and focused training, the Army National Guard defended and protected the base with extraordinary grit. Soldiers from New Jersey as young as eighteen fought off a highly organized and highly proficient attack with no American casualties because they understood their enemy and knew exactly how and when to engage them. I could not have been prouder of their service and determination to protect and defend the mission of the United States Armed Forces.

The enemy of America is real, and it's already here. We can no longer ignore the enduring power of hate or pretend the outlandish divisiveness hasn't been orchestrated by a very specific ideological agenda. We must acknowledge the threats, take appropriate measures to fortify and protect ourselves, and then fight back. Our language must be clear and direct when opposing people who make no excuses for wanting to fundamentally change and destroy this nation. We must be resolute, just like those National Guardsmen, in our dedication to understand our enemy and use it to fiercely protect freedom. Our collective failure has been to allow complacency and political correctness to dictate how we conduct ourselves in words and deeds. We are a nation on a hamster wheel, breathless and exhausted from the effort of avoiding cultural, political, or interpersonal land mines. We have lost our sense of togetherness because the enemy has taken great care to exploit our goodness as a people and the freedom granted to us by God. But not all is lost. We can reclaim that sense of belonging if we stand together and actively resist the lies of the enemy; when we don't allow ourselves to be ruled by the mob. By nature, we are a people who have overcome and persevered through difficult and hopeless times. As much as I hoped we could, I don't believe we can go back to what we were. I think longing for days gone by instead of constructing a new future for our children and grandchildren only delays the immediate action required to move forward. There can be no doubt it will be difficult. The road ahead will not be easy, and it will take sacrifice and courage to stand for what's right. They have grown overconfident in their schemes and have exposed themselves for who they are and what they believe as brazenly antithetical to American principles and values. History tells us we've been here before, underestimated and seemingly outnumbered. But time and time again, history also reveals that the heart of an American who loves freedom and is willing to fight for it is unstoppable, immovable, and resolute. If I were the enemy, I would be terrified.

FREEDOM
BEFORE UNITY

Keeping a Republic is a messy business. Those of us who've been paying attention live with a feeling of foreboding—this is not the America of our childhood. We see clearly that the division and ugliness gripping our country are no longer the birth pains of a young nation. Those times have come and gone, leaving behind prosperity and opportunity unlike anything the free world has ever known. There's something so significant happening that it feels more like seismic shifts, and most people sense the ground quaking along the periphery of their daily lives. This overarching feeling of uneasiness, that our country is no longer morally or physically a safe place, competes with the spirit of freedom we've carried with us like a talisman. We treated it like a charm, a plaything, and the fight to control it has manifested in the most shocking displays of radicalism the country has seen. Freedom is now wielded like a weapon in public spaces instead of respecting its place as the cornerstone of a civil society. The freedom to live your life in a way that honors your values is now completely dependent on someone else's truth. It's astounding, but even in that, many want to find a way to work toward common ground. How do we unite as a nation? The hard truth is unity cannot exist when freedom is perverted. As much as we want to find a way to live in harmony, with the extreme and pervasive ideologies influencing our children and our justice system, I don't think now is the time. At least not until common ground is based on common sense and human decency. Achieving unity in this current environment means one of two things: people either stop living in delusion, or the other half has no choice but to acquiesce. If there has ever been a time to choose sides, that time is now.

We talk about unification and how to resolve some of these big issues bordering on a national crisis, but we can't agree on what qualifies as unity. Competing definitions are fraught with political undertones, making the process of finding common ground that much more polarizing and complicated. Honestly, I think we're at a point where most people believe it's untenable for the country to come together in a genuine way purely because of the lack of intellectual honesty. I've even heard people say it would take another 9/11 to regain that same spirit of unity and patriotism that drew us together on 9/12. We accept that while those first few days were raw, they were also painfully and beautifully real. Our collective grief gave us perspective, and that perspective revealed our fragile humanity, ultimately exposing a truth we often avoid. We need each other. For many months after, no one was a stranger; we were all connected by sorrow, faith, and, yes, righteous anger. We were all Americans. But no one really wants that. No one hopes for bloodshed just to experience a blessing. But I do understand, however misplaced, the longing to regain that same kind of connection to our neighbors. To see someone raising an American flag in front of their business or across an overpass because silently acknowledging we were strangers sharing the same experience was a powerful thing. And as an aside, going to war in that same spirit was a comfort the generation before us was robbed of, reinforcing the importance of unity for those who choose to serve for freedom's sake. There's a real possibility we're too far gone, even for that, the pendulum having swung too far left. But for the sake of our children, I'd rather try and fail than stand by and watch the country I dedicated my life to become a shallow husk of what she used to be.

Half the population says *agree with us and we'll bring you into the fold*, while the other half says *leave me alone and we'll get along just fine*. One side wants to unequivocally define what is tolerable, and the other has been so tolerant they've forgotten what it means to have a voice. But we are no longer people who want the same outcome even though this is exactly what unity is: unity is diversity with harmony. It's not every woman, man, and child agreeing to live under an umbrella of sameness for the sake of peace. Unity is not equivalent to or the definition of utopia. The end goal of perfection is how we've gotten ourselves into this mess in the first place. It is the influence of Marxism and socialism that pushes the narrative that if we all sacrifice a little, everyone can live in equal harmony and there would be no more economic or societal struggles. It's a tired lie that continues to fester and spread in some of the most elite circles in society but finds a receptive audience with disillusioned young people who are longing for purpose. The exhaustive effort has been to create a perfect union instead of a *more* perfect union. The difference being one is unattainable and the other acknowledges the importance of the pursuit rather than the outcome. At the highest levels, results are being engineered and manufactured to create preordained outcomes. It is acceptable thievery, and we see the consequences being played out in real time. There can be no unity in this way of thinking, only dependency, because within that dependent relationship exists a natural hierarchy, making it impossible to inspire genuine loyalty or unity. Inevitably, the dependency manifests itself in an attitude of victimhood and resentment, creating a chasm in both societal and interpersonal relationships. It sacrifices freedom on the altar of equity, and it is the cause of mass disillusionment toward the American dream. We must choose to honor freedom above the misguided notion of equal outcomes for all people. If we strive for national unity without prioritizing freedom, our Republic will not survive. If unity is not possible, then our only other choice is to fight for freedom.

Protecting freedom means unapologetically standing for truth. Not long ago, we lived in a world when our populace was united by two basic, fundamental truths that helped bridge the gap between most idea groups. First, almost all Americans believed in God or the concept of a god. This was vital because it meant the individual felt connected to a higher power and operated from a moral or ethical foundation they perceived as bigger than themselves. It is its own form of self-regulation and personal accountability. Second, Americans believed strongly that the United States was exceptional and expressed it openly and without reservation. The embodiment of both national pride and a perceived, if not real, moral foundation have always been an accurate barometer of our health as a nation. Although imperfect, we worked tirelessly to break barriers and earn our place in the world as its superpower. Now, the methodology has changed and the moral compass that kept us moving forward has drastically stunted our ability to grow. In fact, we continue to move backward in areas of policy and practice as witnessed by the recent explosion of homelessness, poverty, and crime, a stunning regression after many years of progress through dedication and ingenuity. Unfortunately, morality is now fluid and national pride deemed fascistic. The breakdown of these two previously unifying principles alone should be enough to conclude that common ground may not be possible at this time. And if we are unable to unite, then I believe our position is simple. Those of us who believe in truth and freedom for all people must be completely united against those who actively promote and proclaim the end of the great American experiment. Our voice must be so loud the platform of hate and divisiveness no longer effectively influences the direction of our country.

In the face of blatant racism, indoctrination, and calls for violence, our line in the sand must be unyielding and unwavering. It means under no circumstance should we unite with anyone who advocates or practices the medical mutilation and castration of children. This lunacy, where we pretend this is unlike the gross mutilation of girls in third world countries, must end and it must end now. Uniting behind a financially and politically motivated movement that has no qualms leaving children barren, disfigured, and at long-term risk for severe disease is not an option. There is no common ground when we're talking about the physical and mental well-being of children. The only appropriate reaction is outrage, and it should motivate us to oppose any group or government-appointed entity advocating for these abusive practices. We should be offended by the mere suggestion to unite or find common ground with any group espousing anti-Semitic, anti-white, anti-Asian, anti-faith, and anti-family rhetoric. That includes politicians, universities, colleges, and entire nations. Black Lives Matter, specifically, boasted each of these exact same beliefs in their charter before quickly removing them from their homepage during the riots of 2020. Conservatives were called bigots and racists for opposing BLM and their national movement, when in reality, we simply believed them when they told us who they were: a racist, Jew-hating organization that vowed to destroy anyone or anything associated with whiteness, including the nuclear family. They are the very same group who, after the October 7 massacre in Israel, displayed public solidarity for Hamas on social media by posting a picture of a paraglider with the words "I Stand with Palestine." When the blood of children hadn't even dried in the Kfar Aza kibbutz, Black Lives Matter proudly doubled down, solidifying their long-time position that Palestinians "will do what they must to be free." I will not unite behind people who justify a race war under the guise of liberation and decolonization, buzz words meant to ignite a woke base of feeble-minded followers. There is no compromising when it comes to eliminating an entire race of people; Americans have fought and died for that cause multiple times, and I hope we never have to do it again. In the face of certain global war, it's time we unite to reject manufactured oppression and end the cycle of hate.

The first line of defense in this war on truth and freedom is to focus on the two things we can be united in daily. First, we must be willing to individually speak truth when lies are perpetuated in public or private. We no longer have the luxury of silence; the fear of ridicule isn't a good-enough reason to remain quiet when the lies leave devastation in their wake. If we accept the reality that truth is often offensive to the listener, it makes defending freedom that much easier. Let's be the voice of reason and the return to normalcy where being offended is often a part of life. And if reason is not an option, speak truth anyway. Our kids are watching. Trust me, those who advocate for separate spaces based on color, race, or gender don't care about your feelings, and they certainly aren't concerned about being offensive. Don't allow fear, or even empathy, to become an excuse for not standing for objective truth. If we are going to use truth to promote the necessity of freedom, we must first do so at home. There is nothing more important to the success and well-being of our nation than thriving, united families. A family unit that has an inherent sense of wholeness will do more for mankind than all the politicians in the world combined. I cannot overstate how valuable the relationship with your spouse and children are to the health of our country. I'm talking about adults and children who live in a home where they can acknowledge their flaws, cheer each other on, and learn to fail in a safe and loving environment. Not striving for perfection but for purpose. If that family unit is only yourself and your child, your role is that much more important, but it is no less valued. And if we believe that strong families are key to our enduring freedom, then truth must unite us in helping families who are struggling to provide a safe and stable home. I will forever be grateful to the Fitzgerald family, who took in my family after we came to the States and offered us the simple gift of a safe place to call home. They understood that supporting our family would have generational consequences, and how right they were. Their generosity of spirit laid the groundwork for my entire life in America, and I've spent every day paying back their kindness with my service to country and community. This is what real unity looks like when put into practice.

Being a part of something greater than ourselves is a desire so intrinsic, so intimately written in the code of our DNA, that we're willing to do almost anything to belong. Even if you don't believe in God, there is no denying that connection to a higher purpose and people is a vital part of who we are. We'll join the military, fire department, or police department for that connection. We play sports and sit in stadiums on Sundays wearing team jerseys for that feeling of togetherness. Some even don masks, raise a fist, and scream obscenities just to be a part of something bigger than themselves; the need to belong is that powerful. Regardless of motivation, our human nature longs for commonality and community. Even the vilest hate groups somehow forge an atmosphere of acceptance and belonging. We make the mistake of assuming rhetoric is the glue that holds people together. But I contend, for better or for worse, it's the sense of belonging that keeps people anchored to those around them. But like any relationship, if you become unmoored, suddenly drifting because of conflict or dis-connection, that's the moment rhetoric, ideology, and values falter. Once the sense of belonging is fractured, even the tiniest fissure can cause someone to question their belief system all because the bonds of connection have been tested. This is why it's imperative to have absolute transparency in the parent-child relationship. This is how imparting agendas on young children changes a nation. On the flip side, it's also the reason young adults seek anything or any-one, even anti-American groups on colleges campuses, to belong to. We see this and ask how we can possibly reunite as a nation, but the answer, incorrectly, comes full circle to politicians and elected officials, which, to me, is indicative of how we perceive our role as individuals in society. When we collectively believe one man or one party can save our nation from ruin, we're essentially giving up our power as individuals in a free society. Bold, decisive leadership is important, and setting the example from the top can certainly encourage unity. But the layers between you, your family, and the President of the United States or Congress are so deep there is no relational connection strong enough to promote unity in a trans-formative and lasting way. Because of distance, their role, both figuratively and literally, is strictly one of reinforcement. In fact, I would argue the broader the government's reach into our daily lives, the more divided we've become as a nation.

Let's first tackle the foundation of unity and where it's learned, emulated, and practiced. Family, and again the parent-child rela-tionship, is a significant and unique factor in building societal unity. Don't allow yourself to be convinced otherwise. Parents, you have a fundamental right to raise your children in a way that honors your family, faith, and values. Whether those values align with a government entity or school board is irrelevant. The intent and motivation of any third party will never completely align with yours because that's not how they were designed. In fact, the overt political agendas influencing schools, and yes there are multiple, are in direct opposition with what many parents believe is acceptable, age-appropriate dialogue in their own homes. These alternative narratives guarantee children are put at odds with their parents during vulnerable developmental stages of self-exploration and, depending on the age, their ability to naturally experience the cognitive phase of object permanence. Children are being asked not only to distinguish perception from reality but to then commit to a reality based on a narrative they can't fathom and most likely counters the direction and instruction of the parent. A child's sense of belonging begins at home, not at school, and certainly not by people—even those well intentioned—who have no legal or moral responsibility to the long-term physical and emotional welfare of the child. The family unit is the first and best teacher and must function as a whole instead of being carved into wedges at the hands of education activists. That right is yours, not a right given but one certainly threatened and eroded over the past several years. If we want a future return to unity, it must begin now at home. Before we can expect progress on a national level, we must prioritize on a personal level.

The future of the United States lives in your home, eats at your table, and is desperate for you to engage. I've seen my share of parents wringing their hands at the state of our country while their kids sit in their rooms bent over a cell phone. Many of society's challenges are preventable, but we're facing a crisis of expectations. Despite the desire to engage, I think parents have come to the realization that they've given away their power. That's how strong cancel culture has been in America. I see parents who won't engage their kids on topics like anti-Semitism or the anti-faith movement in general. They either don't know how to or want to avoid conflict altogether when kids need them to engage the most. I get this sense that too many parents believe they're doing their children a disservice by instilling in them a value system that may be contrary to the culture. Like it will make it harder for them in the world or with their peer group. But our kids are going to get their values from somewhere, so we shouldn't avoid imparting wisdom from an informed worldview. Otherwise, our kids and young adults are left to fend for themselves and create a sense of belonging in their own way. This is exactly why activism has become the lifeblood of this generation. They want to make a difference and belong to something bigger than themselves. We didn't give them anything to believe in, so they found it on their own. American parents either became so focused on chasing a prosperous future or surviving until the next paycheck that kids fell in love with artificial connection and built a separate version of their life around it. And although they're surrounded by constant stimulation and feedback, they seem uninspired and indifferent. They've been exposed to so much content they don't know what and whom to believe and are left to wade through the onslaught of information without the benefit of a solid baseline of knowledge. At this point, even adults seem confused, yearning for unity, but the yearning seems more steeped in sentimentality and nostalgia than a willingness to work toward that end. If Americans aren't willing to teach and celebrate freedom, which is the foundation of unity, then we can't expect the next generation to become united in their love of country by happenstance.

Parents, your kids are more connected to influencers than they are their siblings, grandparents, or cousins. They are forming their worldview from an equally confused and frustrated peer group. They need us to teach them what to love and cherish and why, but instead, we hand them an online encyclopedia authored by radicals and agitators who've taken it upon themselves to rewrite history. They crave the affection and attention of strangers more than they do their own family. One of the main reasons we're losing our connection to one another has everything to do with the glowing rectangle in our hands. If unity's the goal, then intentionality must be the priority. You can't be one voice out of literally millions competing for their attention and headspace. In today's world, it's not enough to want to be the most important influence in their lives, you must earn it and sacrifice for it. And even during the teenage years when they naturally distance themselves and friendships compete for your time together, our kids still need intentional engagement and compassionate wisdom. It's time to reevaluate what connection looks like in your home. Do they understand you belong to one another? Have you made your family the priority before sports, friends, and other outside influences? I know that concept is taboo now: everyone lives for sports, and parents spend years dividing time and going in oppositive directions between kids and fields only to get to launch day and wonder where the time went. Is home reliable, predictable, and safe? All qualities that solidify their place in your family unit. If technology and apathy have a stranglehold on your family, if your kids are more content looking in the eyes of a two-dimensional stranger than the people who love them, you may have traded connection for easiness. If you aren't the intentional influence in their life, someone else will fill that space in their heart and mind, and they'll most likely fill it with lies, confusion, and bias. Home is where they learn about community, and belonging is what will give them the confidence to go into the world as adults with an inherent sense of purpose.

The disconnect between parents and their children is one of the greatest threats we face as a nation. This generation is more anxious, depressed, and suicidal than ever before because too many are floating through life untethered. It may not seem like they've been encouraged to live separate lives online, but the moment we gave them access to the internet and social media without boundaries, we gave them permission to unplug from the reality within their four walls. What they're exposed to online is addictive and mesmerizing, and you can't compete on the same level. Kids and teens shouldn't be spending hours online making videos or commenting for likes and follows. They should be watching little sisters play soccer on the weekends or learning family recipes with their grandmas after school. They should be raking leaves for an elderly neighbor or hanging out with friends where there's eye contact, laughter, and smack talk between pizza and driveway basketball games. They should know all the words to "America the Beautiful" and volunteer at church or summer camp. They should be digging in the yard, fishing, and making up games out of sheer boredom. We should be encouraging them to find solutions to problems right in their own backyards, cheering and working alongside them as they find a passion and purpose for their life. If we want unity, it starts by giving them ownership within the family. It looks like accountability and teamwork because a family can't function when only one or two people do the heavy lifting. As soon as our kids could stand on their own two feet, April had them in the laundry room, pulling damp clothes from a basket and throwing them in the dryer while they sang songs together. In our house, plates and bowls are always in the lower cabinets so the kids can help unload the dishwasher no matter their age. It helps them learn the pride of accomplishment, and it normalizes hard work and sacrifice of one's time. We pray for our neighbors, we thank veterans for their service, we send the kids to help a mom with her newborn trying to load a basket of groceries in the rain. Our boys hold the door for their sisters and mom. When my oldest joined the Boy Scouts, I taught him the youngest Scouts always eat first and as a leader he should always eat last. All these are such little things, but they encourage intentionality. They also help inoculate against a natural tendency of self-centeredness. These small efforts will make them more likely to go into the world not so focused on themselves that they miss the people around them who need encouragement or help.

If we're going to focus our efforts at home, we should be teaching our kids what we believe and why. It's important to teach them to respect another person's opinion, but in today's world, it may be even more important to help teach them how to identify the difference between the truth and a lie. So much of what they hear or are going to hear may be sprinkled with facts but is so infused with emotionality and bias that it warps the message completely. Make no mistake, the sole purpose of this tactic is to intentionally deceive. This constant appeal to emotion will be this generation's downfall if we aren't deliberate in guiding them how to objectively receive and process information and distinguish right from wrong. This doesn't happen by accident. Discernment takes time and practice, and it won't happen outside your home, so don't rely on others to impart this wisdom. We should also be actively teaching our kids that being easily offended means being easily controlled. They need to know that being triggered by the words or beliefs of a person who happens to be in close proximity is indicative of a morally weak and corruptible person. A strong mind is capable of objectively questioning information that may not align with their personal belief system without offering abuse in return. It also means having the courage to question your own convictions before settling on a belief system using logic, reason, and faith. It takes quite a bit of faith for some of these people to believe what they do, so don't be afraid to instill faith in your own children. If anything, they should have faith in their ability to stand up for their convictions and know that you'll be right there beside them. Young people must have a strong base of knowledge to be able identify half-truths and lies, but they continually lack an unbiased, well-rounded education, making it that much harder to counter highly cultivated and selective misinformation. A well-trained mind will seek wisdom, in this way making truth a priority above what is considered popular or tolerable.

April and I spent many nights lying awake talking about the next move or deployment, anticipating the tears and reminding ourselves why it mattered to press forward. Unless you've been through it, it's hard to describe the dichotomy between service and sacrifice, especially when the child sacrifices for the service of the parent. It was hard to hold on to unity when time and distance were our family's battlefield. There have been moments of guilt and sorrow, anxiety and fear. It didn't always feel fair, and there were many times we questioned whether we were doing right by them, the constant upheaval a steady topic of conversation once the bedroom door was closed. People boast of the resilience of military kids, and they're absolutely right, but we had an obligation to constantly revisit our family's decision to serve knowing a cohesive family unit was critical to their future. We know that our role as parents is bigger than just raising little kids; we're raising future adults, and our choices affect not only our family but yours too. Our adult kids will one day go into the world, and their childhood experiences will no doubt influence how they operate in society. It was incumbent upon us to prayerfully and purposefully reevaluate our motivations for their best interest. For me, serving our nation in the United States Navy was how I demonstrated my love for them. Serving our country and her people was a love letter I wrote them every time I walked out the door and promised to come back. We wanted to be the ones who showed them that life is a journey of choices motivated by sacrifice for others, even people we don't know or always agree with. That our duty extends beyond our home and can even reach the farthest parts of the earth if we're brave enough. We wanted them to see that courage was doing hard things even when it hurt as much as we wanted them to be surrounded by people who believed the same, that our way of life was worth fighting and dying for. We knew there would be pain, but we also knew there was value in fighting together through some incredibly difficult moments. April and I often struggle to find balance between sharing the reality of the world we live in and focusing on the role of being the helper. During our time on active duty, when it felt dark and friends died or marriages fell apart, the only thing we knew to do was recommit to each other as a couple and as a family; near or far, for better or worse, in sickness and in health. We chose not to turn our back on the hard times, instead facing our trials with truth, faith, and an abiding love for one another. We knew the greatest gift we could give them was to teach them to always stand for what's right, to never back down in the face of evil, and to protect those who cannot protect themselves. Our job isn't to withhold hardship or pain from them but to walk beside them. And when it feels overwhelming, our simple but gentle reminder to them is that we belong to one another. *Team Cao all the way.* This is how we still get through the hard times, and I think it's a similar sentiment our nation must eventually adopt in order to unite.

Before our feet touch the ground in the morning, after we've prayed and thanked God for the breath in our lungs and one more sunrise to love our people, we should take a moment to ask ourselves one very important question: *Am I a person worth dying for?* It's important because the fight is here for soul of our nation, and these seven words may give us the perspective we need to meet the challenges ahead. For those of us who served, we did so because our family and our country meant more than our own lives. They were worth the risk of dying young, surrounded by people who hate us. We fought, we bled, we came home broken. We went so you wouldn't have to. Were you worth it? We left pregnant wives and dying parents. We missed recitals and teaching them to drive. We left in the early morning hours without goodbyes and came home after birthdays, anniversaries, and holidays had been celebrated in our absence. Were you worth it? Our kids learned to be brave when all they wanted was to be a normal family who didn't spend years apart. They put their hands on their heart and stood quietly at attention because it meant feeling close to us while we were thousands of miles away carrying a folded flag in the stinking desert because the stars and stripes reminded us of home. And not just home with family, but the nation that counted on us to fight without question in a place long forgotten. We wrote letters and tucked them safely in a drawer in case we didn't make it back. Our greatest fear was being forgotten when the years passed by without us. I hope you were worth it.

Any chance we have for our futures rests in us being worthy of a stranger dying and fighting on our behalf. When we're ready, and I hope that day is sooner than later, this is how we'll find common ground. We won't find unity in politics, and it won't be because of fanatical rhetoric on either side. There will be a return to common sense when faced with our differences so the voices of division can mostly recede and no longer find a relevant platform. We'll know when that day comes because we won't care how we identify, the color of our skin won't dictate our personal narrative. We'll choose to live far more dangerous lives for the sake of others regardless of our occupation or disposition. We will rediscover dignity in work that brings us neither fame nor riches. Children will leave, but they will come back to strengthen and grow the family unit, once again normalizing multigenerational communities. And finally, character will qualify us before preferential status, and the only box we'll ever need to check is the one marked "American."

ACKNOWLEDGMENTS

The past twenty-five years have been filled with the greatest and most challenging moments of my life. I have experienced tragedy and triumph and will carry the scars of war and service with me forever. But I've learned that God uses it all for His good and I recognize, even in the midst of truly difficult experiences, that I have been blessed more than I deserve. April and I keep our eyes focused on fighting for a better future for our five children, all of whom have borne military life and its aftermath with grace and courage. It is for them, and the future of our nation, that we do hard things. We love you kids, and hope you know that you are the reason we serve, and you are the reason we continue to fight. Team Cao forever.

This book wouldn't have been possible without the love and support of our family and friends. You have supported us unconditionally and encouraged us when the road seemed too long and filled with too many obstacles. At every turn, with every new idea and new endeavor, you've graciously just known that the *Cao family is at it again*! Just another crazy addition to an already hectic life, and you've loved us through every wild step of the way. Your testimony has been your relentless and faithful dedication of prayer for us, and we couldn't be more humbled. Thank you for loving us so well and cheering us on every step of the way.

To the Navy Deep Sea, Explosive Ordnance Disposal, and Special Warfare communities, I want to honor your years of friendship, sacrifice, and loyalty. It was a privilege to serve alongside you as quiet professionals on the front line of irregular and asymmetric warfare the likes of which the world has never seen. You embody tenacity and grit, and our country is better for your integrity and steadfast commitment to preserving life, even at the risk of your own. To those we have lost, may we never forget. Let our place in a world without you be a reminder to the next generation that the cost of great loss is to live a life worthy of your sacrifice. I know I speak for all of us when I say that we strive every day to be good stewards of your legacy. And finally, to the walking wounded: always beside you, brothers.

Our sincerest thanks to Al Regnery and his team at Republic for taking a chance on us. It's not every day you get to tell your story, and Al's quiet confidence gave us the freedom to tell my story in our own way. He believed in our message, and we hope, because of his faith in us, that it honors those just like me and my family who overcame incredible adversity in the face of death and destruction. We were an entire generation of men, women, and children who fled war only to be embraced and accepted by the greatest nation on earth. I hope our collective experiences are a reminder to Americans that prosperity is not a promise but a purpose. Religious, economic, and social prosperity are available to all because of American freedom, but it must be safeguarded and protected.

ACKNOWLEDGMENTS

Finally, to my wife. Without you, this book would never have been written. You were able to take my linear engineer's way of thinking and compose this masterpiece. You are gifted beyond belief with your words and the way you tell a story. You are my best friend and my rock. God sure knew what He was doing when he united us twenty-five years ago, and I look forward to the next twenty-five, my love.

ABOUT THE AUTHORS

Hung Cao arrived in the United States in 1975 after escaping Vietnam days before the fall of Saigon. Hung and his family settled in Virginia before quickly moving to west Africa where he spent most of his youth. At the age of twelve, Hung returned to the States to pursue an American education, later earning acceptance to Thomas Jefferson High School for Science and Technology's inaugural class. He entered the United States Navy as a Seaman Recruit and went on to graduate from the United States Naval Academy with a Bachelor of Science in Ocean Engineering in 1996. Hung earned a master's degree in Applied Physics at the Naval Postgraduate School and is a Fellow from both the Massachusetts's Institute of Technology Seminar XXI for US National Security & Foreign Policy and Harvard Senior Executive Leadership.

A Bronze Star recipient, Deep Sea Diver, and Explosive Ordnance Disposal Officer, Hung conducted high-profile salvage operations including the recovery of John F. Kennedy Jr., the Civil War Ironclad USS Monitor, and servicemembers killed during military operations. Hung commanded the Naval Diving and Salvage Training Center, and as a Master Explosive Ordnance Technician, he commanded various teams rendering safe IEDs on the battlefield and at home. Among them was the Combined Explosives Exploitation Cell in Iraq, a multi-national, multi-agency counter–Improvised Explosive Device team. During his last combat deployment in 2020–2021, Hung was the Director of Counter-Improvised Threats for Afghanistan. Hung served numerous staff tours, and his final assignment was with Defense Threat Reduction Agency, where he created and led the Operational Effects Division (J3X) for Sensitive Activities, Exploitation, Counter-Unmanned Systems, Joint Expeditionary Teams, and counter-messaging. Hung retired after twenty-five years of service to his beloved adopted country. He is currently a Vice President at a Fortune 500 company.

Hung became the GOP nominee for Virginia's tenth congressional district in May 2022 after sweeping a crowded eleven-way primary. He believed integrity should be the cornerstone of politics and committed to being a standard-bearer so Virginians, as well as all Americans, could be proud of their leadership in Washington. Hung believes that service begins with sacrifice and continues his fight to restore common sense in politics at the national level. Hung co-wrote, wrote, and published several op-eds on education, meritocracy, and national security with the Washington Post, the Washington Times, the Washington Examiner, and Fox News.

As a member and guest speaker for the United States Naval Academy's Minority Association and Diversity, Equity, and Inclusion Forum, Hung consistently drives the conversation towards diversity of thought, encouraging Midshipmen to avoid using their minority status as a crutch or excuse for personal or professional failures. Hung recognizes that leadership in our armed forces begins with self-discipline but ends with a cohesive fighting force that does not bow to cultural or political ideology.

Most importantly, Hung is the proud father of five children and has been married to his wife, April, for over twenty-five years. They have endured the hardships of war and politics together, relying on faith and family to inspire, encourage, and fight for the future of their children.

April Lakata Cao was born and raised in Northern Virginia. As a writer, she has devoted herself to encouraging families in faith as they strive daily to strengthen their relationships in parenthood and marriage. April was a proud contributing author to the award-winning book, Faith Deployed...Again (Green, J., Moody) and has been published in Focus on the Family's Thriving Family Magazine along with numerous popular online publications. April has been a ghost writer for several op-eds published in the Washington Post and Washington Times. April finds great joy in being a wife to Hung and mother to five beautiful children. She began homeschooling ten years ago to better serve and support her children during the upheaval of military life and numerous combat deployments. After eleven moves in seventeen years, they settled and made a permanent home in Purcellville, Virginia. When she's not writing, April serves as a first responder in her community. Her role as a volunteer Emergency Medical Technician compelled her to begin studying Social Work at Liberty University in order to meet the growing mental health needs in the field of Crisis and Trauma Intervention.